ANTIQUING
and
COLLECTING
on the
INTERNET

Karima Parry

COLLECTOR BOOKS
A Division of Schroeder Publishing Co., Inc.

DEDICATION

When I was a little girl, my father would come to tuck me in at night, and instead of telling me bedtime stories, he taught me about business and economics — convertible debentures instead of trolls and fairy princesses.

This book is my way of thanking him.

And for my adored husband Aziz, who will complete what my father began.

Cover design: Beth Summers
Book design: Karen Geary

SEARCHING FOR A PUBLISHER?

We are always looking for knowledgeable people considered to be experts within their fields. If you feel that there is a real need for a book on your collectible subject and have a large comprehensive collection, contact Collector Books.

COLLECTOR BOOKS
P.O. Box 3009
Paducah, KY 42002-3009
www.collectorbooks.com

CONTENTS

INTRODUCTION

Before the advent of the Internet, antiques buyers had to be a brave dedicated lot. They had to be willing to make great efforts and endure all kinds of discomfort and hardship in pursuit of their treasures. Instead of sleeping in on the weekends, they had to get up at the crack of dawn to be the first at garage sales, yard sales, house sales, tag sales, and church bazaars. They often had to drive long distances to places obscure and unknown to trek through antiques shops. They stoically soldiered on in searing heat at vast summer flea markets laid out on sizzling expanses of asphalt parking lots. They trustingly sent their money to total strangers in response to ads for items sight unseen in antiques newspapers. They were forced to sit perfectly still on uncomfortable folding chairs or even stand for hours at auctions. They haunted the thrift and second hand stores, and spent endless hours combing through junk.

The heartiest among them thought nothing of traveling great distances, paying for food and lodging, and then slogging through ankle-deep mud before sunrise at Brimfield, Massachusetts, and at other antiques sales around the country. Some enthusiasts stood in line for hours so that they could be among the lucky first ones through the gate at shows. And for the truly battle hardened, there were always the Pier Shows in New York City, and the enormous Atlantic City and Cow Palace shows. And the worst part of all of it was that antiques seekers often came home frustrated or empty handed either because what they wanted was not to be found, or when it was found prices were beyond their reach or desire.

And it wasn't much better for sellers. They spent hours tagging every single item for a garage sale, yard sale, or house tag sale. If they elected to put their merchandise in antiques malls, sellers had to pay rent on their space, and often a commission on their sales. They had to stock and clean their booth, and they could not depend on mall staff to be knowledgeable about their inventory. Selling through monthly antiques flea markets or swap meets meant that they had to get up in the middle of the night and drive to a location where they were required to be set up by 4 a.m. Then they had to swelter all day under a flimsy umbrella or small awning where the ground temperature was 130°. Or, when they weren't getting heatstroke, it was freezing cold or it rained all day. Those who sold through antiques shows had to transport their inventory to a show and back again, at great effort and expense, and with no guarantee that they would sell enough to even meet their expenses.

Real world auction houses were a more comfortable way for sellers to sell, and buyers to buy, but when a seller put their items in auctions they had to give the auction house a hefty piece of the action, and increasingly auction houses are charging a buyer's premium above the hammer price as well. If a piece failed to meet its reserve, then the piece had been publicly humiliated and the seller would have to stash it away for awhile or get it out of town until people forgot about it and it could be brought back out and re-auctioned.

Sellers who had antiques shops struggled too. They were burdened with all the usual overhead costs which made profitability especially difficult for low volume lower end dealers, and those shops which are located in out of the way places. In other words, from the perspective of both buyers and sellers, the time was ripe to explore other ways of conducting the antiques business, and the Internet arrived at just this moment in time.

Thanks to the Internet, these days buyers and sellers can conduct their business from the privacy and comfort of their homes or offices at whatever times are convenient for them. Regardless of the season or the weather, on the Internet the antiques season is

12 months a year, 7 days a week, 24 hours a day. Buyers can browse with their collections, reference libraries, and price guides at their elbow. They can comparison shop without ruffling feathers, and without their buying being scrutinized by others as happens sometimes at shows. Dealing on the Internet offers both buyer and seller a heretofore nonexistent level of convenience, selection, and privacy.

An astounding array of antiques of every possible type and origin from every corner of the world can be found on the Internet. There are numerous venues and ways for sellers to sell on the Internet, and buyers can choose whichever forum feels most comfortable for them. Some buyers prefer the excitement of buying through online auctions, while others deplore the undependable nature of online auctions and the lavish amount of time that the buyer must spend combing through listings. Many of these buyers prefer to do their buying from websites. From contacts made in chat rooms, through Listserves, bulletin boards, and private deals; no matter which venue they choose an antiques buyer will rarely have to come home from a cyber-antiquing session empty handed.

Selling antiques on the Internet has many of the characteristics of a dream job. Sellers can choose their working hours, they have minimal overhead, and the Internet provides them with an almost unlimited audience of eager potential buyers. They don't need to tie up their money in a shop full of inventory, as even a single piece can be easily and readily sold on the Internet. It doesn't matter where buyer or seller are located, as long the seller can receive buyer's payment and the item can be shipped from seller to buyer then business can be transacted. In short, the Internet is the best thing that ever happened to the antiques business for both buyers and sellers.

The growing commerce in antiques on the Internet is beginning to exert a disconcerting effect on many real world casual antiques venues including flea markets, tag sales, and thrift stores. Reports from all over the United States suggest that now that there is a reliable way for almost anyone to market small antiques through Internet auctions, nice small antiques are disappearing from these kinds of venues. Antiques seekers are seeing a general decline in the quantity and especially in the quality of antiques found at these casual selling venues as much of the items are being picked and then auctioned on the Internet. The pieces that remain at these places are either overpriced, not of interest, damaged, too fragile, or too cumbersome to ship. The chances of finding treasures at these casual venues are dwindling.

The Internet is responsible for many changes in how business in general is being conducted around the world, and will have far reaching impacts of all sectors of business in the future. This book will specifically consider the micro example of how the Internet has impacted the antiques business. As the action in antiques commerce increasingly moves to the Internet, it is critical that antiques buyers and sellers learn to navigate the Internet confidently so that they can utilize this valuable new tool to their own advantage. By understanding how Internet antique commerce works, and by gaining insight into the motivations and concerns of both buyers and sellers, all readers whether they are buyers or sellers or both will learn what they need to know for them to participate confidently and successfully on the Internet.

THE END OF REGIONALISM

Prior to the Internet, regionalism was a significant factor in many aspects of the antiques business. It existed in terms of buyers' access to antiques for sale; the availability of certain kinds of antiques for sale; in antiques pricing in general; and in regionalized markets which had established their own pricing structures regardless of prevailing prices in other areas of the country. The greatest virtue of the Internet in terms of the antiques business is that it has effectively leveled the playing field by allowing buyers from anywhere to compete on equal footing with each other for items, and by allowing sellers from anywhere to compete with other sellers. The Internet has created a truly global marketplace, where the item speaks for itself and both buyers and sellers meet in a forum that is without local boundaries or local influences.

Antiques commerce on the Internet is continuing to expand, and the Internet is rapidly becoming the main forum for buying and selling lower to middle level small antiques. Eventually Internet prices will become the benchmark pricing structure for most antiques in this range. If recent deals made between some of the most respected auction houses in the country and a few of the major Internet auction sites live up to their potential, then it is possible that the market and future prices for some better to high end pieces will eventually be established on the Internet as well.

Availability of antiques has always been spotty around the United States, with some regions far better supplied than others. Those who lived in areas where there were not a lot of antiques, such as sparsely populated rural areas, had a harder time finding them or collecting them than did buyers who lived in or near to metropolitan areas. As pickers and others passed through rural areas, they bought whatever there might have been that was worth buying. So, anything of value headed for the cities and even less was left for local enthusiasts.

In addition, certain kinds of antiques have tended to be more plentiful in specific regions of the country. Pressed glass, for example, was far more available in New England than in other areas of the United States. And, the majority of pressed glass collectors were also clustered around the New England region. If a collector in Los Angeles, for example, wanted to buy pressed glass, their opportunities to build their collection locally were considerably more limited than those of the collector who lived in Boston.

There are two central reasons why certain kinds of antiques were regionalized. The first is that antiques have always tended to be more plentiful around the areas where they were originally produced. This explains the continuing availability of antique art pottery in and around the Ohio Valley, where much of it was made. The second reason has to do with the local tastes of buyers, who were usually predominantly from the local vicinity surrounding a shop. Smart dealers tailor their stock to conform to local tastes and trends as these determine how well certain kinds of antiques compliment their local esthetic. For example, a Louis XIV piece that had somehow made its way to a shop in Maine or Montana could languish there for years. In New York City, this piece would be sold in a heartbeat. New Orleans antiques buyers have always reflected the historic French and Southern cultural influences of the region. Dealers who sell to buyers in this city service the regional taste with fine old silver and porcelains, which enjoy great popularity in New Orleans, but which can be difficult to sell to buyers in some other areas of the country. Retro kitsch from the 1950s may have begun its revival in Miami and New York, but it is still a pretty hard sell in the Midwest. So, local shops have always had to consider local tastes and preferences in stocking their shops.

In the past, buyers or collectors whose demands were not met in their regional market had little choice except to travel to antiques shows, go to auctions, or seek other ways to shop for antiques outside of their region. Although retail shop sellers will continue to have to consider local tastes and demands in their choice of stock, thanks to the Internet their local buyers are no longer restricted to what is available locally. Dealers, too, can take advantage of the non-regionality of the Internet as they now have the ability to sell items to buyers from outside of the local area.

Eager buyers will no longer be stymied when they have cash to spend and can't find what they want to buy locally. It is pretty safe to say that if it exists in real life, it exists somewhere on the Internet, and accessibility to antiques for sale is now the domain of everyone everywhere. The only thing limiting any buyer will be the size of their wallet.

Prior to the explosive growth of antiques commerce on the Internet, prices for many kinds of antiques were spotty and uneven across the country. The reason was that they were reflecting higher or lower supply and demand in certain areas or regions. Although dealers have always operated under the classic market determinants of pricing based on what the prevailing market will bear,

*"...If it exists in real life,
it exists somewhere
on the Internet..."*

their prevailing market was primarily a localized one. So they priced their items in keeping with norms within their local market. Local economics and local demographics were important factors to include in pricing structures. In areas where there were fewer potential buyers, and those who existed had lower disposable incomes, dealers could not expect to move their merchandise if their pricing did not take those factors into account. Equally, sellers in high-traffic, high-income areas were unashamed to take advantage of local buyers by pricing their merchandise higher than average because that is what their localized market would bear.

The net result of this situation was that an item that retailed for $750 in Boston or Chicago could be had for $350 in Pittsburgh or Cincinnati. Savvy pickers and others who were able to travel ferreted out items from out-of-the-way shops in smaller cities and at country auctions. Many of these items eventually made their way from the periphery to the big cities on both coasts, where big city dealers acted essentially as middlemen. They would buy the piece from the picker and stock it. Eventually, they would resell it for the lion's share of the profit.

Guides for prices realized for items on Internet auctions are readily available on most Internet auction sites. They are updated constantly, and rarely become obsolete as quickly as do printed price lists. This information is accessible to everyone. Buyers and sellers can easily determine price levels for any category of item by researching completed auctions archives on any of the online auction sites. Obviously auction hammer prices can have ups and downs as bidding wars drive some hammer prices to unrealistic levels, or lack of participants with an interest in a certain item can result in its closing at an unrealistically low price. However, reviewing these prices will give users a price range which will help them to place their item in context. They can then augment this information with visits to websites to check prices on similar kind(s) of items. In the end, they will get a good idea of what they can expect to have to pay for a piece, and what they can reasonably expect to get for selling it. Sellers who sell on the Internet are practically forced to consider Internet price trends and to price their items accordingly.

An excellent example of the effects that the end of regionalism-based pricing is having on antiques would be to consider the example of Bakelite jewelry. Real world Bakelite dealers in New York City had gotten used to paying some of the highest acquisition prices in the country for their items, and they were used to selling them and getting some of the highest retail prices in the country too. In effect, the New York City Bakelite micro market determined buy and sell prices for this group of dealers in this particular commodity. Buyers and sellers there had become accustomed to dealing with each other and their customers based upon these prices.

For the last few years, quite a few New York City Bakelite dealers have listed some wonderful Bakelite pieces on eBay. The majority of these pieces, however, have gone unsold as the reserves are completely out of equilibrium with prevailing Bakelite prices on eBay as set virtually daily by the hammer results on similar items. As of this writing, New York City Bakelite dealers are discovering that Internet selling prices for Bakelite jewelry are usually significantly lower than the New York City retail prices that they are used to. New York City Bakelite dealers will have to bite the bullet and bring their prices in line, or they will lose customers to other dealers on the Internet who are willing to sell comparable pieces at a lower price.

Some sellers from outlying areas are finding that they have another unexpected advantage over big city sellers on the Internet. Often these sellers have lower acquisition costs for their items. They may find that Internet prices may be higher than what they were able to get for their items locally. However, some sellers from certain regions are not finding the Internet as beneficial for their sales. Sellers from areas where local prices for antiques are high, such as sellers located in large metropolitan areas, are at a distinct disadvantage. It is difficult for these dealers to compete against sellers who bought less expensively and who are willing to sell less expensively too.

Not only do some dynamics of local markets loose saliency when the Internet is factored into the equation, but the effects of the Internet filter down to impact on local markets. Pricing as determined by hammer prices on eBay may actually impact the localized New York City market and cause Bakelite prices there to fall somewhat as they head for parity with Internet prices. The only good news for New York City Bakelite dealers is that after getting used to paying stratospheric prices, shopping on the Internet, especially from the online auctions, looks like the Bakelite bargain sale of all time! This condition is not limited to dealers in Bakelite or dealers in New York City, but it affects dealers in most specialized categories of antiques who are located in large metropolitan areas.

Despite the impact of the Internet, some pockets of regionalized pricing will remain awhile longer in areas such as New York City. This is because dealers there who have bought locally may have had higher acquisition costs than dealers from other areas. Some of the retail customers who will continue to buy from these dealers have not yet taken the leap to cyberspace, and will continue to accept the local pricing structure as it exists. But it is only a matter of time before they get brave, get online, and abandon their local dealers in the name of finding better bargains on the Internet. Over the long run, these dealers will have to take some losses if they want to be able to sell competitively on the Internet or even continue to successfully retail their merchandise within their local market.

The advent of the Internet has thrown retail dealers into competition not just with other dealers on their block, but with other dealers around the world. As the Internet establishes antiques prices equilibrium and relatively predictable national/global market prices for antiques emerge, retail dealers will have to bring their prices into line or risk having to eat their merchandise. On the

Internet every seller is competing for buyers, and not just with all the other shops on their street or in their neighborhood, but with every other antiques seller around the world who has access to the Internet and something to sell. Non-dealer sellers compete head to head with the top dealers. Until dealers price their items in line with prevailing Internet prices, non-dealer sellers might enjoy an added advantage in that their asking prices for items do not include much overhead, and they are often willing to accept a lower percentage rate of profit. The micro economics of locale where the item was acquired by the seller or where it is being sold are meaningless on the Internet. The buyer doesn't care who or where the seller is. The item will speak for itself, and will sell for a price that truly reflects a global market value for that item.

The Internet has created a lively global marketplace where all online sellers are free to offer their merchandise to all online buyers, and all buyers have equal access to items for sale. In the free market tradition, supply and demand and the quality and characteristics of the items themselves dictate prices. Thus, the effects of regionalism on prices, availability, and markets have been removed from the equation. The net result is that although some aspects of regionalism will continue to exist in a few isolated pockets, on the whole the Internet is effectively bringing regionalism in the antiques business to an end.

As the Internet rapidly destroys the saliency of regionalism and the those factors connected to it, it is being replaced with a truly global free marketplace. This new globalization of antiques commerce offers unprecedented opportunities for some, and some surprising negative impacts for others. As with all sweeping changes, there are winners and losers. But by understanding the positions and concerns of the various stakeholders in the antiques business, both buyers and sellers will be in a better position to benefit from the opportunities that this unprecedented globalized antiques market has created, and to minimize risk and avoid losses.

WHAT DOES THE INTERNET HAVE TO OFFER?

THE VENUES

The Internet offers various resources. They include e-mail, chat groups, Usenet news groups or list serves, and websites. These and others resources that the Internet offers provide many different options for antiques buyers and sellers. Each of these venues has pros and cons, and depending on whether you are a buyer, a seller, a collector, or just curious, some of these options may be better suited to your needs than others. However, before reviewing the variety of venues in which antiques buyers and sellers can do business on the Internet, and which ones various buyers and sellers may find the most appealing, it is useful to discuss precisely why the Internet is such an attractive option for antiques buyers and sellers, and why it will grow to dominate antiques commerce well into the future.

To begin with, the Internet operates without interruption. Your local Internet service provider (ISP) may go down from time to time, but not the Internet itself. It is always out there, and always operational. The world of the Internet is always available. The Internet has virtually unlimited capacity. It may slow down or operate sluggishly when stressed with an unusual volume of traffic, but on the whole, it will always be able to accommodate as many who want to use it. On the Internet, time is not a factor. Anything on the Internet is accessible every day of the year and around the clock. The Internet doesn't close down for vacations or have legal holidays. The Internet is convenient. You can use it at a time that is convenient for you, from the privacy of your home, or your office, or at school, or anywhere else where a computer and an access provider is available. The cost is very reasonable. Although there are many websites which do charge money for the client to participate fully in whatever they are offering, the vast majority of sites are still free, and will probably remain so. Thus, the only cost to the user is in their equipment, telephone line for their modem, and Internet service provider fees. The Internet is vast, and expanding rapidly as new sites are being added daily.

E-MAIL

E-mail is electronic mail. It can be sent across the room or around the world in a fraction of a second, and it's free (except for your ISP charges). You can send text, photos, music (if you and the recipient have the proper hardware and software) of any length, to any other person who has an ISP and an e-mail address. All e-mail addresses consist of a username@domain.com, or username@ domain.net, etc. The @ sign is read as "at." E-mail addresses which end in ".gov" are government related. Those which end in ".org" are organizations. It is critical that you enter e-mail addresses correctly, including special attention to letter cases. Mistakes can lead to lost mail which never reaches your intended recipient and is not necessarily returned to you as undeliverable.

"The Internet...you can use it at a time that is convenient for you, from the privacy of your home, or your office, or at school, or anywhere else where a computer and an access provider is avaiable."

E-mail etiquette has developed as e-mail has proliferated. Typing with all capital letters is considered to be the equivalent of yelling. Also considered rude are sending or forwarding unsolicited junk mail or unwanted chain letters to others. You should alert a recipient when you are going to send them an overly large file, because sometimes their mail account may not be set up to receive large files. The result will be that their mail account will freeze up and refuse to deliver all their mail that has arrived after yours until they contact their ISP to unclog it. Just because you are writing on the Internet, it does not mean that good grammar, spelling, punctuation, and general good manners are not relevant. Quite the opposite, as how you present yourself to others through your e-mail is how others online will view you. Finally, it is generally expected that e-mail, especially if it is business related, should be answered within two days of receipt. Since lost mail is not always returned to the sender, if you do not reply to your mail in a timely fashion, the sender has no way of knowing whether their mail ever reached you or not.

CHAT GROUPS

Chat groups are everywhere on the Internet. They are a venue where from two to hundreds of people can chat with each other by typing and sending notes simultaneously in real time. Some of the larger groups can be intimidating for new users as when they first arrive and find that there are often several conversations between several different users on several different subjects going on all at the same time. Newbies can feel like they just can't get a word in edgewise. Some people feel too shy to just jump right in. But that is how to begin, and if you let others in the group know that you are new at this, usually they will be understanding and help you along. After all, they were once newbies themselves. Another thing that some people dislike about chat groups is that everyone in the group will see everything that they say. The remedy for this and other concerns are private chat rooms.

PRIVATE CHAT ROOMS

Private chat rooms are created when one or more people open a location for a room, and then invite those with whom they wish to talk to come to that location and join in. Private chatting can be great fun, as you get to discuss whatever you want without the entire chat group looking over your shoulder. However, do not operate under the assumption that everything you say in a chat room is confidential, or that every person you meet in a chat room is telling the truth. Use common sense and remember that you really have no idea who you are talking with, whether they are being completely honest with you, and whether they are sharing your conversation with anyone else.

Chat groups can be great fun for specialized groups within the antiques community. Not only can you meet others who share your interests and who are eager to discuss it, but you can also ask other members for advice and mention your website (if you have one) or items that you are trying to sell or looking to buy. They are a quick way to make new cyber friends with the same interests as yours, in real time.

USENET GROUPS AND LISTSERVES

Usenet news groups are electronic bulletin boards where members can "post" comments which are then read by everyone in the group. Listserve posts do not utilize a bulletin board. Instead, postings are forwarded individually to every person on the group's mailing list. Unlike real time chat rooms, Usenet users can view the bulletin board at their convenience, and listserve members can read the posts they receive as they arrive in their mailboxes or open them at their leisure. Members of either group can reply individually to the original poster or comment on the post to the entire group.

Each group specializes in a single topic, but in general these topics are quite broad and often posts are only loosely related to the stated topic. There are in excess of 35,000 Usenet and listserve groups available on the Internet at any one time, and many of them are available that discuss antiques. This particular venue is also an excellent way for you to meet people who have similar interests to yours, to exchange information about that interest, and to make contacts which eventually may lead to buying or selling or other activities within your sphere of interest.

Some members are very active, posting messages often and corresponding with other group members. Others "lurk" by reading bulletin boards or receiving postings but rarely post anything themselves. Most listserves have a core group of people who may have been involved with that listserve for several years or more. Other members subscribe and unsubscribe at their convenience.

Every Usenet group or listserve has their own rules for participants. When you sign up to participate in one of these groups, your confirmation usually includes a FAQs (Frequently Asked Questions) sheet. It is a good idea to familiarize yourself with it before leaping into the group. Some Usenet groups are very businesslike and prefer for postings to discuss the topic and topic-related issues only. Some listserves tend to be looser, becoming giant electronic clubs where users feel that they know each other well enough that postings often include jokes, birthday wishes to members, and other personal communications which are not strictly speaking relevant to the topic. As a result, some listserves receive so many postings that you may find yourself wading through acres of e-mail with little of interest in much of it.

If you become a member of a large popular listserve, you can find your mailbox inundated with mail that can number several hundred pieces per day. Some browser programs have a way that you can set up your system so that incoming mail from the listserve is delivered to its own folder, effectively eliminating the need for you to sort your mail manually. However, without that feature, the mail from a listserve can get overwhelming and cause you to miss non-listserve mail at times. If you are not able to access your e-mail frequently, listserve mail can pile up and fill your mailbox to capacity. Any additional mail that arrives after your mailbox is filled will be returned by your mail provider to the sender as "undeliverable." So, if you are going away, even for a few days, it is a good idea to unsubscribe to your listserve. You can always re-subscribe when you return.

Usenet groups and listserves are a wonderful place to ask for help in identifying something, or some other technical issue that relates to the group. Unlike chat rooms where your resources are limited to whoever is online and participating at the moment when you ask your question, on a listserve your question will go out to every member of the group. Some may post an answer to you immediately, others may respond to you once they have gotten their mail and read your posting. However, the resources of the entire group are available to you, and you never know who else is in your listserve. These groups attract individuals who want to learn as well as some of the top experts in each field who are knowledgeable and willing to share what they know. Many experts that you might otherwise not have access to participate in listserves. Especially for newbies to antiquing on the Internet, participating in Usenet groups and listserves are one of the smartest things they can do.

WEBSITES

Websites are pages on the Internet that are reached by entering their correct address. This can be done manually by clicking on "open" then entering the address, or by clicking on a link which automatically takes you to that address. Most website addresses begin with "www." Links begin with "http://www." Websites run the gamut from educational, promotional, commercial, entertainment, and political to personal pages and more. A recent development are websites which include live camera coverage of some event or individual in real time. The important thing to remember is that site addresses can be confusing and typing them in accurately is critical.

There are several kinds of websites which are of special interest to antiques buyers, sellers, and collectors. They include Internet auction sites, catalog sites, antiques informational or educational sites, online antiques mall sites, antiques clubs or organizational sites, and more.

Internet Auction Sites

There are a growing number of Internet auction sites, but some of them will be more useful to you than others. It is relatively easy for a company to open an auction site. The hard part is attracting a sufficient number of sellers and an audience of buyers. Sellers have much more at stake in Internet auctions than buyers do. If a seller bravely lists a few items on a new site just to try it out, they risk tying up that item for the duration of the auction. When the item closes, they may discover in the end that their items either did not sell or sold at a disappointing price. The key for Internet auction sellers is to sell only on established Internet auction sites where there is already a large audience of buyers who are looking for what you have to sell. In my opinion, as of this writing, a seller's best place to sell is eBay, period!

This may or may not always be the case. New Internet auction sites are appearing daily. Their goal is either to fragment eBay's nearly 6 million person audience or to attempt to peacefully coexist with eBay while offering buyers and sellers an alternative.

"...best place to sell is eBay, period!"

There are a number of methods that these new auction sites are using to solicit your participation. Some begin by offering free listings as an incentive to attract sellers. Some agree to waive hammer price fees, again as an incentive to sellers. It is the strategy of "give it away today so that you can charge for it tomorrow." But unless many sellers take the plunge, and a sufficient number of buyers find and participate in the site, even these early starting-out-in-business incentives may not be enough. If there are no buyers or hammer prices are low, the sellers will abandon the new auction site and return to the auction site(s) where they have done well in the past.

Some new Internet auction sites are trying to attract specific segments of the antiques market. They reason that rather than go after such an enormous market as the jack of all trades eBay, why not target their efforts at a specific market share or niche? So, there are Internet costume jewelry auction sites or collectible glass auction sites or Beanie Babies auction sites, etc. If you're a Beanie Baby enthusiast, then perhaps this might work for you, but rather than substitute it for eBay, you may want to use a specialized auction site to supplement your other Internet auction options.

Some Internet auction sites work in slightly different ways than eBay. Some do not permit sellers to list items with a reserve. Others have a feature that the auction only begins once an item has received at least one bid. Another twist is that some auctions have an automatic extension on the closing times on their auctions. Instead of bidders worrying about jumping in at the last minute, each time a bid is received on the item in the closing moments of an auction an automatic time extension is activated, and bids for that item will continue until no bidder elects to bid any further. The benefit for buyers is that they do not have to worry about being outbid in the closing seconds of an auction, and then prevented by the clock from entering another bid. The benefit for sellers is that their item will not close until everyone who wants to bid on it has had an opportunity to do so.

Another kind of Internet auction site which is springing up is that in which retailers are using the auction as a virtual outlet store to retail their goods. Unlike auctions where opening bids are much lower than the retail price and there can be many bids and bidders, sellers on these auctions need only one bid for them to walk away happy. The sellers who sell on these auctions often are listing brand new goods, and pricing opening bids at the lowest price they are willing to sell them for — which is usually a small percentage below retail.

Some antiques sellers use the same tactic one eBay, with mixed results. Auction buyer mentality combines the search for items they want, along with the hope that they will acquire them at a bargain. Antique items which open with retail opening bids tend to discourage bidders. Especially in such a highly competitive environment as Internet auctions, buyers are likely to ignore auctions with very high opening bids in favor of bidding on auctions where opening bids are reasonable with the hope that the reserve, if any, is reasonable too.

As watching the hammer prices for antiques sold through Internet auctions and reviewing pricing structures on websites will quickly demonstrate, the price of an antique anything is not a fixed price, but rather a range of prices within which the item will fall at that particular time and on that particular site. This depends on many factors including the quality and characteristics of the item itself, the site where it is being sold, what the seller's acquisition cost was on the item, how badly the seller needs money, what "the books" say the item is worth, the time of day that Internet auction item is closing, even the day of the week can matter sometimes as not everyone is willing to spend their weekends or holidays planted in front of a computer screen. The bidding on Internet auctions allows all these factors to determine where within the range the price will fall at that given time. Sometimes a buyer can get lucky when for some unknown reason or other no other bidders show up to bid against them. Other times, the price on an item can inexplicably spiral out of sight as two bidders fight it out to the end. Despite Internet pricing on various categories of antiques which can be watched and tracked, there is always an element of uncertainty to buying and selling on Internet auctions. There are no sure things, and sometimes there are surprises both good and bad for buyers and sellers.

"...the price on an item can inexplicably spiral out of sight as two bidders to fight it out to the end."

Online Catalog Sites

An online catalog is a website that features color photos, descriptions, and prices of items for sale. These are virtual shops which are open 24 hours a day, 7 days a week, 365 days a year, and can get an unlimited number of potential customers per day. There are more than 150,000 antiques related websites on the Internet as of this writing, with new ones being added daily. Some of these websites get thousands of visitors per week and become successful. Combined, they do millions of dollars worth of business per year. Successful sites attract a loyal clientele that visit and buy from them regularly as well as thousands of visitors. Others languish in obscurity.

As an antiques enthusiast, finding catalog websites in your interest area will not only provide you with more opportunities to buy, but will also increase your knowledge about your area of specialization. Some of these catalogs will include informational articles, or a virtual exhibit, or items of this kind that you have never seen before. Some will provide links which will take you to other sellers in the same field or to resource sites. In addition, you can write to the site owner if you have something they might want to buy or to ask questions. As many sellers save their better pieces to sell from their websites rather than in Internet auctions, smart antiquers on the Internet shop from websites as well as the Internet auctions.

Other Sites of Interest

The power of the Internet for researching antiques is infinite. It puts the greatest research library ever assembled in the history of the world at your fingertips. If, for example, you would like to learn more about an antique Wedgwood teapot, or the Wedgwood company in general, there are many useful sites which will come up on the search engines. They will include Wedgwood collectors' societies; museums which have pieces of Wedgwood in their collections; sites which discuss the history of the china industry in Great Britain; auction sites which will give you prices realized for Wedgwood in their auction archives; china collectors' newsletters; sites selling both old and new Wedgwood; and many more. By skillfully conducting your searches, you can probably find out whatever you want to know.

THE SEARCH ENGINES:
How to Find What You're Looking For

In terms of sheer magnitude and power, no tool on the Internet is more useful than the search engines. When effectively used, they can literally unearth a needle from a haystack. Many users do not utilize search engines effectively, and they miss out on many sites that may be of interest to them. In this chapter, you'll learn the hows and whys of using search engines, including creating effective initial searches, and then distilling those searches using advanced searching techniques and search refining techniques. The Internet is vast, and there is no table of contents. Learning how to use search engines to sift through the almost limitless amount of information available is crucial.

Search engines search through incredible amounts of data at more than lightspeed to locate whatever the user has asked them to find. The many search engines on the Internet range from those which search within a very discretely defined area to those which search the entire Internet. There are mini-search engines which will search only within the site where they are provided. Some search engines are topic-specific. For example certain search engines will only search for medical-related topics. Some sites, such as many of the ISPs (Internet service providers; like AOL, CompuServe, etc.) provide their own search engines. These engines will search from a specially constructed list of sites, often comprised of businesses who have advertising agreements or other business links with those individual ISPs. In essence, when a client uses a search engine such as these, they need to realize that they are getting abbreviated results. In addition, the searcher can be almost certain that ISP search engines are programmed to rank their paid advertising clients to appear within the first few hits generated. Still, these search engines can be used by some searchers who are not looking for a comprehensive list of hits. For example, a searcher who wants to know what the weather is in Bermuda only needs to find one hit out of the thousands available. Conversely, those who are searching with hopes of getting many hits, such as antiques browsers, may be disappointed by the limited nature of search results generated by ISP search engines.

For searchers who are looking for broad-based initial results, the major search engines such as Hotbot, AltaVista, Lycos, Yahoo, and the newly-launched Google are a better choice. Their searches are the widest, and all of these search engines present their findings in descending order ranked by how well they match the original search criteria. They all also offer various features which can aid the searcher to augment or narrow down the initial search results.

To begin with, searchers need to learn to distill their initial searches down to one or more carefully chosen keywords which are as unambiguous as possible. Then, the searcher must understand how to present these keywords to the search engine so that they get the maximum effective result. When quotation marks are placed at each end of a keyword group, such as "Antique Sand-

"Search engines are your most important Internet tool. Practice searching, and you will discover many surprises that otherwise would have escaped your attention."

wich Glass," they tell the search engine to search for exactly those words that are enclosed inside the quotation marks in the order that they are presented. When no quotation marks are placed around keywords, some search engines will turn up any site that matches or relates to any one of these keywords, or any two of these keywords, etc. This can result in search results which are not at all what the searcher had in mind.

When searching using the following keywords *antique Sandwich glass,* I got the following number of hits on each of the major search engines: Hotbot: 200 matches; AltaVista: 364,970 web pages; Lycos: no total number of web pages specified, but page after page of hits; Yahoo: 1,833 web pages; Google: 2,526 matches. (Remember that search engines are constantly scanning the Internet for material and new material is constantly being placed on the Internet, so the search results above were obsolete five minutes after I found them.)

It can be inferred from these results that AltaVista pulled in by far the greatest number of hits, suggesting that AltaVista's search logic is the broadest of the five. Hotbot, on the other hand, only came up with 200 matches. However, they were tightly focused and generally were about antique Sandwich glass, as opposed to glass sandwiches or antique sandwiches. Yahoo and Google were within the middle range, with Google finding roughly 25% more matches than Yahoo.

Conducting a successful search depends on a number of factors, but most important of these is how precise the user has been able to make their search criteria. The trick for users to understand is that broad search criteria will yield far more results than they can possibly go through, as shown above. Those search results will likely include many extraneous or non-relevant results. A good example of this is the staggering number of hits generated by AltaVista when I searched for *antique Sandwich glass* which included countless hits for restaurants and sandwich shops along with other sandwich-related sites. It also included an avalanche of antiques sites, not all of which might deal in Sandwich glass. Finally, it yielded innumerable sites about glass or which are glass-related but had nothing to do with antique Sandwich glass.

You may want to make your initial search even broader by introducing more keyword terms such as *Boston*. However, the keyword *Boston* would generate many irrelevant hits, as does our original search keyword *Sandwich*. By placing these keywords together as in *Boston + Sandwich,* this asks the search engine to search for these words occurring together. (The company which produced Sandwich glass was known for a time as the Boston-Sandwich Glass Company.) On one hand, you will get hits for sandwich shops in Boston, but on the other hand, your likelihood of turning up Boston-Sandwich glass hits is enhanced. Later, you can eliminate unwanted hits from your search results.

Another suggestion is to take advantage of the adjacency feature of some search engine's logics framework. This allows you to search by adding keyword terms such as *hand-blown, opalescent, molded,* or *stippled* to your original search keywords. These are all technical terms which relate to early glassware manufacture or characteristics of early glassware and would likely appear adjacent to and therefore possibly related to your earlier search keywords, increasing the possibility that the engine would find them for you. For example, if the search engine finds a site where hand-blown is mentioned, it is likely that this site has something to do with glass. Searching by adding some or all of these adjacent terms may turn up sites that the initial search did not pick up.

Now that the big initial search has been done, and you realize that you don't have the time or energy to go through thousands of results, it is time to learn to narrow the results through advanced search refinements such as inclusions and exclusions. Although the search engines allow you to search again from their entire search field, or from within your initial results, I have generally been satisfied with narrowing the search field to that which is included in my initial search results.

An inclusionary search refinement allows the searcher to refine their query by adding more precision to how the search engine utilizes the keywords. For example, if the user were primarily searching for a Sandwich glass lamp, they might want to introduce *lamp* in their keyword search. This can be accomplished by using a plus sign so that search would be *antique Sandwich glass + lamp.* However, this will still turn up a lot of irrelevant hits. Putting quotations around some of the keywords, however, will make this search very precise: *"antique Sandwich glass + lamp."* This way, the search will only turn up lamps which are antique Sandwich glass, and not just antique lamps or lamps which are made of glass.

Finally there is the exclusionary search refinement which allows the searcher to add modifications which tell the search engine what hits to remove from the list. This is accomplished by adding a minus sign to the keyword string, so that search would be *"antique Sandwich glass − food."* This would get rid of most of the sandwich restaurants and other food-related hits. The same logic can be applied to exclude modern glass manufacturers, etc. from the final search results.

Another critical skill for searchers is creativity. Sometimes, by restating the search keywords results may be better. In this case, when I restated the keywords from *antique Sandwich glass* to *glass antique Sandwich,* AltaVista turned up a staggering 1,806,550 web pages. This is roughly five times the number of web pages found when searching the keywords in the first version!

Search engines are your most important Internet tool. Practice searching, and you will discover many surprises that otherwise would have escaped your attention.

THE SELLERS

The Internet provides a marketplace where everyone is welcome to sell. The Internet makes it possible for all sellers to expose their item to a limitless audience of potential buyers. Sellers all over the country are either abandoning the real world venues where they used to sell or supplementing their real world venues with Internet sales. But virtually instantaneous liquidity is not a foregone conclusion. Sellers must be able to decide where they should sell on the Internet for the most effective results. Each selling venue offers different costs and benefits, and choosing the proper selling venue is critical. Each seller has their own reasons why one venue might be preferable over another. Even if you are only interested in buying on the Internet, understanding sellers' concerns and psychology will help you to buy more effectively.

Those who sell antiques can be divided into several categories, and some sellers overlap two or more categories. Each seller has their own reasons why they have chosen to sell an item, and each seller operates with a slightly differing set of constraints and expectations. By breaking down sellers into the following general categories, we will get some insight into who is selling on the Internet and why. The categories include casual sellers, generalist sellers, picker sellers, specialist sellers, consignment sellers, dealer sellers, and collector sellers.

CASUAL SELLERS

In the past, many casual sellers utilized garage sales, flea markets, and tag sales to sell their items. However, those can be a lot of work and are not a realistic option for sellers who only have a few items to sell. Some casual sellers have so much to sell that the benefits of renting space in an indoor flea markets are obvious. For a nominal overhead, these 12-month-a-year operations allow hundreds of casual sellers to clean out their basements, garages, and attics, and then put the items in a permanent location for sale. Serious antiques are rarely found at these venues, but you never can tell, and many antiques buyers check out places such as these regularly.

Many casual sellers have attempted to sell through newspaper ads. Local papers give their ad local exposure whereas a national publication, such as one of the high-circulation antiques weekly newspapers will give their ad national exposure. Many of the national antiques weekly newspapers used to be filled with ads from casual sellers. However, since the advent of the Internet, the number of casual sellers selling through these ads both nationally and locally has diminished. Internet auctions have made it easy for casual sellers to sell online, and casual sellers are increasingly choosing to sell their items themselves on the Internet. An added bonus is that their item will often be sold more quickly through an online auction and at a lower cost to the seller than through newspaper ads.

Without utilizing digital cameras, scanners, and the lightning speed of the Internet, deal making with a casual seller can turn into a long, drawn-out affair while photos are taken and sent out for developing, letters are sent by regular mail, etc. Even when sellers and buyers resort to the telephone to work out a deal, the deal can take weeks to come to fruition. For obvious reasons, this is not quick enough to suit many sellers or impatient buyers.

Sellers and buyers both have reasons to be leery of conducting business through newspaper ads. Although sellers can insist on money orders for payment or depend on their bank to clear checks before the item is shipped, there is always the chance that they could end up with a problem buyer. Some unscrupulous buyers have attempted to defraud sellers by various methods, and some sellers have been victimized. In addition, some buyers have been defrauded by dishonest sellers who either misrepresented the item, its condition, or its value.

Buyers, too, take significant risks as they send off their money. If an item arrives and it is unsatisfactory, some buyers have had a nasty surprise when the seller suddenly cannot be contacted. Some unhappy buyers attempt to enlist the aid of the newspaper in which the ad originally appeared, only to be told by the newspaper that they are not in any way responsible for transactions that result from ads in their publication. The unhappy buyer is left with no recourse other than reporting the seller to the post office and lodging a claim against the seller for mail fraud. Because of these pitfalls and others, the number of people willing to buy from or sell through newspaper ads has always been somewhat limited. Although many transactions from ads are successful, the stories of people who have had bad experiences conducting business this way are legion.

Another Internet option for casual sellers is posting for sale notices on various bulletin boards on the Internet. However, the selection of a bulletin board should be done thoughtfully as some bulletin boards get far more exposure than others, and some are more appropriate than others. If the seller advertises their item on a specialized bulletin board that is devoted to that kind of item they have a better chance of finding a buyer than if they advertise

"...eBay and other Internet auction sites are tailor made for the casual seller. Internet auctions provide them with a dynamic marketplace where their item will be viewed by buyers who have a specific interest in that kind of item."

it on a general bulletin board. In addition, some of the general bulletin boards, such as the ones run by ISPs, have an enormous number of postings and there is a high likelihood that their post will not be noticed.

Since casual sellers usually have only a few things that they wish to sell, they do not have sufficient inventory to open a website. None the less, some casual sellers elect to open a website. Sometimes these websites are in Internet antiques malls. However, the fact is that casual seller websites are rarely successful at selling items. One reason that they rarely do well is because casual sellers often do not maintain their site. They just put it on the Internet and wait for buyers to come. The casual seller does not know how to advertise or promote their site. They rarely replenish it with fresh merchandise or remove stale or sold items. Their sites can look very unprofessional with pictures of things that have little to do with the items being sold. In short, they are not professional sales people who are eager to turn customers into repeat clients. Visitors who manage to find their way to these obscure websites usually click out of them almost immediately once they discover that they are offering only a few items for sale, and if they return some time later and discover the same few items, they will delete this address from their bookmarks or favorites list. Overall, the best venue for casual sellers on the Internet are the Internet auction sites.

Casual sellers who sell on Internet auctions are neither sales professionals nor antiques professionals. Many casual sellers already sell on Internet auctions. However, they often lack the facilities to take good pictures of their item and their descriptions can be confusing and inaccurate. Sometimes their reserves are wildly optimistic, as are their opening bids. Despite these shortcomings, eBay and other Internet auction sites are tailor-made for the casual seller. Internet auctions provide them with a dynamic marketplace where their item will be viewed by buyers who have a specific interest in that kind of item. Their audience will include buyers who are knowledgeable about the sort of item that they are selling and who will be able to recognize the item from their description and/or photo. In the end, the chances are good that the item will be sold. These auctions are easy to participate in, and the costs are minimal if the seller lists and sells the item themselves.

One of the most frequently voiced concerns about doing business on the Internet is that buyers and sellers who do not know each other do not have any backup in the event that the transaction is unsatisfactory for one party or another. There is no question that certain venues on the Internet provide a safer environment than others for both buyers and sellers to conduct their business. Buying from a website is only as reliable as the individual who owns that site. But it is not easy to check on the reputation of a website dealer. If that dealer belongs to a professional organization or group and advertises so on their site, this can provide the potential buyer with a way to ask for references on a seller. Websites that specialize in a particular kind of antique are usually owned by individuals who are well known within that specific antiques community. It is likely that you can ask around to see if others in that specific antiques community have had any dealings with that website and whether they were satisfactory or not.

Some Internet auctions, through their customer service areas, ostensibly provide the parties with some backup in the event of problems. Although most auction sites strictly adhere to the policy that they are facilitators of the sale, but not involved in the sale, they can be extremely helpful if they are willing to intervene when problems develop.

GENERALIST SELLERS

Arguably, shop owner sellers whether they are generalists or specialists may be in the most disadvantaged position of all sellers since the advent of the Internet. They continue to have all the usual financial burdens associated with retail sales, and they are responsible for all the chores which are necessary when operating a walk-in retail establishment. Depending on their location, their opportunities to sell are, for the most part, still confined to their local market. Although many buyers are abandoning combing the shops in favor of doing their antiquing on the Internet, not all shops are losing all of their clients. Shops in high traffic areas can fare better, such as those in locations which benefit from seasonal tourism. But on the whole, unless a shop is well located — in or near a high traffic area or in an area with a solid regional economy where the antiques market is lively and collectors abound — many shops are often only marginally profitable.

In the last ten years, many generalist shop owners have decided to minimize their overhead by consolidating with other dealers into cooperatives and antiques malls. Others have closed their shops in favor of relocating them in a rented space in an antiques mall. Antiques malls eliminate crushing overhead expenses of running a free-standing operation, and free up dealers to go out buying instead of having to mind the shop. Also, in presenting many dealers together under one roof, the size and convenience of antiques malls is a strong incentive for potential buyers to, in effect, visit many shops all in one trip instead of having to visit each shop individually. By placing antiques malls in high traffic areas, a shop owner will get much more traffic, and more sales, for less overhead cost per sale. At least that is how it is supposed to work.

In reality, antiques malls have been a mixed blessing for dealers. They compete literally head-to-head for sales in malls. Mall personnel are usually spread thin and often unknowledgeable and disinterested in one another's merchandise. Theft is a continuing problem. Too many dealers selling low caliber merchandise can lower the general quality of some antiques malls to the point where middle level and more advanced antiques buyers elect to go elsewhere. The Internet is causing a quiet revolution in antiques malls around the country, where increasingly the items for sale there are those which for one reason or another can not be easily sold on the Internet. Quality of merchandise at antiques malls is plunging, and buyers are concluding that they can shop more effectively and with a better quality and variety of items if they do so on the Internet.

Other generalist sellers have sold their merchandise through antiques shows. Antiques shows have been around since the 1960s. Basically, they are a traveling instant antiques mall. By doing shows, sellers can showcase their items to buyers with sufficient interest in antiques that they are willing to pay an admission fee just to see them. Sellers can utilize shows to network with other sellers, cut deals, and exchange information. They also have the opportunity to show their items to a whole new group of buyers at each show. For buyers living in areas where there are few antiques shops, antiques shows are eagerly awaited and usually well attended. They bring in out-of-town dealers with fresh merchandise that gives local buyers an alternative to what is or is not available to them locally.

Antiques shows have their down side too, both for sellers and for buyers. Sellers who elect to participate in antiques shows must shoulder costs of booth rental, show participation fees, packing and transport of their merchandise, insurance, any extra employees needed to set up the booth and man it for the duration of the show, travel expenses, meals, lodging, etc. Many factors which are beyond their control can turn a show into a disaster where they will not sell enough to recoup their costs. These can include foul

"Quality of merchandise at antiques malls is plunging, and buyers are concluding that they can shop more effectively and with a better quality and variety of items if they do so on the Internet."

weather, time of year, competing local events that are scheduled at the same time, and unforseen local economic downturns. Showing and selling at antiques shows is very hard work, with long hours, constant activity, and virtually no breaks. Theft is a problem which seems to be more prevalent at larger shows, and dealers have to watch their booth carefully. They never know when a "looker" might turn into a potential buyer or otherwise, so everyone who makes an inquiry about a piece needs to be treated as both a potential customer and also a potential shoplifter! People who lurk around but do not make inquiries need to be watched, too. Some sellers who are able to build an easy rapport with strangers can do very well at antiques shows, but many aging sellers are finding that the whole process is more physically and mentally demanding than they are able to endure.

Buyers, too, can find antiques shows trying. Some buyers have traveled significant distances to attend, and they may have incurred travel, food, and lodging costs. Some shows are so huge that buyers can be overwhelmed. Buyers can have problems unearthing the kind of items they seek from the veritable mountain of items available. Some shows feature a wide range of dealers whose inventory runs the gamut from inexpensive items on up. Other shows tend to concentrate on bringing together a certain level of dealers, such as all top-of-the-line dealers at the Armory Show in New York City. A show such as this one has little to offer beginning or middle-level buyers, other than a chance to see items that they would love to have but are not able to purchase. Some collectors who buy at shows are squeamish having their transactions watched by a crowd which can include other collectors or other dealers. Gossip spreads like wildfire at antiques shows, and not every buyer or seller wants their business made known to others. Of late, some of the highest-end collector/buyers are making deals with show sellers over the Internet and then attending the show strictly to pick up their merchandise from the seller.

Some of generalist shop owners are already selling more on the Internet auction sites than they sell through their shops, at shows, or through other venues. However, opening websites is not the best choice of venue for generalist sellers. Buyers can have trouble finding generalist antiques websites. Buyers search for websites by categories and keywords. A search asking for antiques dealers could return in excess of 500,000 hits, and even the most ardent antiques hound will not have the time or patience to go through them all. But a search for antique Toleware, for example, will turn up a fraction of that number of hits, some of which are Toleware specialist dealers. Visiting these specialist-dealer websites is far more efficient for the potential buyer than searching through generalist websites which might include only a single piece of Toleware. This lowers the likelihood that buyers searching for a specific category of antiques would even browse generalist websites. So, in the case of the Internet, generalist dealer websites are at a disadvantage whereas specialized websites are at a considerable advantage.

Online antiques malls are one way that generalist dealers can improve their chances on the Internet. By grouping together from a few to a few hundred generalist dealer "shopfronts" which are all accessible from a single homepage, shoppers who arrive at the site can conveniently click their way from store to store without having to leave the site. These sites will be especially attractive to non-specialist buyers, who are browsing for anything that strikes their fancy, as opposed to a specific category of antiques.

Another venue that can be utilized effectively by generalist sellers are online auctions which include a site specific search engine. Potential bidders can conduct keyword searches which will turn up whatever a generalist seller is selling that fits the keyword, regardless of the category where it is listed. Internet auctions provide sellers with the means to quickly sell off merchandise that might not be salable where they are located or that has become stale or shopworn. These same items could be placed on a website and eventually might be sold, but the time frame for website sales is much longer than that provided by Internet auctions.

Generalist dealers often utilize online auctions as the dumping ground of last resort. That is, as a way to quickly cash out of merchandise that they no longer wish to hold. When they are ready to move an item out, regardless of the possibility of taking a loss on it, they always have the option of putting the item on an Internet auction with no reserve. Unless the item is completely unsalable, the old saying that there is a key for every lock will prevail, and someone will come out of somewhere and buy the item. Those generalist dealers who maintain websites can use their item descriptions in Internet auctions to invite bidders to visit their website where more lucrative sales can be made.

Non-generalist sellers with narrow specializations, such as country furniture, have always worked within their field, and often have lists of clientele with a specific interest in a certain category of antiques. But generalist dealers who deal in a wide selection of antiques cannot possibly compile lists of interested buyers for every single category of antiques that they carry, nor might those buyers exist within the local vicinity of their dealing area or be accessible by shows. So, generalist sellers have always had special difficulties in effectively marketing their items. Now that the Internet is firmly entrenched with both buyers and sellers, generalist sellers have more options for selling their antiques. It appears that the best strategy for the generalist seller is a careful mix of both real world and Internet venues.

PICKERS

Pickers are professional antiques buyers who travel around and buy anything they find that they think they can re-sell as quickly as possible at a profit. Pickers work with a limited amount of cash, and don't want to see their cash tied up for very long in anything they have bought. They want to get into and out of an item as quickly as possible. Although some pickers are highly specialized and search only for specific kinds of items, many of them are generalists who deal in anything from baseball cards to pre-Colombian emeralds. In the past, pickers did not expect to realize large profits on their buys. They were usually content to take a small profit while selling the item to a dealer. The dealer would eventually re-sell the item at retail, and make the lion's share of the profit.

Professional pickers do a tremendous amount of traveling which makes the responsibility of maintaining a website undesirable for them. In addition, there is always the chance that an item on a website will sit and sit with no buyer in sight. This is why pickers rarely utilize websites to sell their merchandise.

Pickers have discovered that the speed and relative liquidity that Internet auctions provide is a much better choice than selling their finds to dealers. Not only do Internet auctions provide a ready market for almost any antique that a picker has found, but they also can give pickers the quick turnover on their items that they need so that they can cash out and keep on buying. On Internet auctions, pickers sell their items directly to retail buyers and collectors. They make more money, more quickly, and they are cutting their former customers, the dealers, right out of the action. Dealers who once bought significant amounts of their inventory from pickers are having to find other sources of antiques. Those dealers who buy on the Internet are having to compete with other dealers for the items that the pickers used to walk into their shops to sell.

"On Internet auctions, pickers sell their items directly to retail buyers and collectors. They make more money, more quickly, and they are cutting their former customers, the dealers, right out of the action."

Although selling through Internet auctions is the best venue for pickers, running their auctions can be inconvenient for pickers who travel frequently and can be too busy to service their auctions including invoicing, receiving payment, and packing and shipping their items. Increasingly, some pickers are utilizing the services of a consignment seller who takes care of Internet auctions for a fee and/or a percentage of the hammer price.

Selling on the Internet gives pickers a level of liquidity and profitability that they have never had in the past. They are no longer obliged to sacrifice much of their profit to dealers. Instead, they compete head to head with them. They no longer are stuck with cash tied up in items that they can't seem to unload. They can always put them in an Internet auction with no reserve and kiss their mistakes goodbye. Finally, picking was never an easy way to make a living, but the Internet has made it a whole lot easier.

As antiques commerce continues to grow, along with demand for more antiques to sell to eager buyers, picking will become more competitive and more difficult. The ease of learning about antiques through books and the Internet along with the ease of selling them on the Internet encourages enterprising individuals to start picking antiques. These amateur pickers are competing with established professional pickers, and the result is that everyone is finding less and less as the real world venues where pickers have traditionally found antiques are being picked dry.

SPECIALIST SELLERS

Specialist sellers are a uniquely focused breed of antiques dealer. These sellers build their entire businesses based on a single type of item and then build clientele from the rather exclusive group of those who are specifically interested in that kind of item. Specialized sellers can be thought of as Internet boutique sellers. They come to be associated in the buyers' minds with the type of item that they specialize in, and buyers know that they can always find items of the type at a specialist seller. In addition, specialist sellers are usually the most knowledgeable about what they sell, and they are often willing to share their expertise.

Specialist sellers are uniquely suited to selling on the Internet both from websites and through Internet auctions. Keyword searches on the various search engines give these sellers a special advantage in that their audience can find them easily and with precision.

Some specialist-dealers create and maintain websites which are cyber catalogs. Unlike real world places of business, these cyber catalogs are open for shopping 24-hours a day, 7 days a week, and have either minimal overhead, or virtually no overhead at all. When the appropriate keywords are used, Internet search engines will

"Some specialist-dealers create and maintain websites which are cyber catalogs. Unlike real world places of business, these cyber catalogs are open for shopping 24-hours a day, 7 days a week..."

readily point interested shoppers to these websites. Some specialist seller websites do a lot of business, but some do not. One reason for this may be pricing. Specialist sellers tend to price their prized items somewhat higher than the general market prices for these items. It is because they are often collectors, too, and feel that the pieces are rare or particularly desirable. As a result, some specialist-dealer websites are a droolfest of killer pieces that are priced to the moon — beautiful to behold but as unreachable (and un-buyable) as the stars.

Some specialist sellers who have websites also sell in Internet auctions where they generally do well. They tend to sell lower end pieces on Internet auctions, while keeping their better pieces for sale on their website. Their item descriptions often include advertising directing buyers to their website or a direct link to it. These specialist sellers view Internet auction sales as a way to advertise their website more than as an important sales venue. They know that anyone looking at their auctions will be interested in what is on their website and that advertising in this manner is virtually guaranteed to reach their targeted audience, no matter how specialized.

Within certain category areas on eBay, for example, various virtual communities have sprung up consisting of buyers and sellers who do business primarily with each other within that specific category or categories of antiques. Auction search engines and category searches quickly guide even the greenest newcomer to the places where they will find items of interest to them. Over time as both buyers and sellers watch the listings in their chosen category(ies) and participate in an auction or two, they come to recognize the regular sellers and buyers within that category. It is not surprising, then, that e-mail correspondences spring up, and personal relationships are formed between buyers and sellers who share a common interest, but who may be located on opposite sides of the country. It is a natural extension of these relationships that an indeterminate number of deals are cut privately between the parties.

CONSIGNMENT SELLERS

Internet auctions have fostered an explosion of consignment sellers. These are sellers who run professional consignment operations online, utilizing online auctions to market their client's items. They broker the sale and service both the seller and their buyer. Unlike generalist sellers, consignment sellers have no investment in the items they sell. Instead, they have a computer, a scanner or digital camera, and are willing to use them to provide a service. The client delivers the object to the consignment seller, who photographs it, writes a description for it, lists it, manages the auction, collects the payment, is billed for auction charges, packs and ships the item, pays the auction charges, and then issues the client a check minus their fees and auction charges.

One inescapable fact is that listing and managing an auction for an expensive item is exactly the same amount of work and effort as listing and managing an auction for an inexpensive item. The net result is that consignment selling is not an economical option for sellers to use to market inexpensive items. By the time the consignment seller collects their fees and auction charges are paid there is almost nothing left for the original consignee. However, for middle range or better items, consignment sellers offer individuals hassle-free access to Internet auctions which can find buyers for their items that they may not be able to find locally.

Consignment sellers generally charge a flat fee, a percentage of the hammer price, or both, and they make their money on individuals who do not have computers or access to them, or the time to list and manage auctions, but who want to sell their items on the Internet.

DEALERS

One of the most worrisome aspects of dealing in antiques is that the dealer ties up money in an item with no idea of when or whether they will be able to resell the item and take their profit. Unlike pickers who buy into an item but then get out of it quickly, dealers are generally into an item for the long haul until a buyer can be found. One fundamental change that the Internet has provided for dealers is that they can choose when to sell a piece, as opposed to having to sit with it until someone chooses to buy it. This discretionary liquidity is changing the way that dealers are running their businesses, and the long haul is getting shorter.

Dealers who have shops or mall spaces know that after a month or two their merchandise starts to get stale as it has been passed over by local buyers. The smart dealer won't hold on to these items too much longer. Even if they take a slight loss, it is better business for them to turn items over so that they can restock with fresh merchandise. Thus, many dealers regularly sell off items they no longer want to keep in inventory by selling them on Internet auctions. The items for sale will be seen by a fresh audience of buyers, and the odds are that one or more of these buyers will be more enthusiastic about the item than buyers were in the dealer's local area.

In general, buying from a dealer through an Internet auction is better than buying from a casual seller. Dealers tend be more knowledgeable about their merchandise, and their descriptions include the information that sellers want to see. Dealers manage their auctions more professionally. They service the buyer and generally back up their merchandise. On the down side, dealers may price their items higher than pickers or casual sellers.

COLLECTORS

Collectors are unique among online sellers. They utilize websites and online sales primarily as a way to groom their collections. As their collection grows and their tastes mature, they utilize the Internet to sell off the bottom-end pieces in their collections. Collectors who do this contribute to the availability of the kind of beginner-level pieces which encourage new collectors to enter that collecting area. Rarely does a collector begin a collection with top-of-the-line examples of their chosen type. Instead, most collectors begin with lower-level items. As the collection grows and the collector becomes more knowledgeable and more discerning, the mature collector outgrows their initial purchases.

Prior to the Internet, liquidity for lower-level pieces was a problem for collectors. They did not always have ways of finding novice collectors who were anxious to buy beginner-level pieces. This was especially difficult for collectors who were not dealers. Maturing middle-level collectors often were stuck having to keep items they had outgrown and no longer wanted. Not anymore! Whatever venue they decide to sell from, there are always novice collectors looking for beginner-level pieces. Middle-level collectors fill that demand by selling off their lower-end items to novice collectors who are delighted to have them. These sales generate cash so that the middle-level collector can keep on buying, usually replacing these pieces with better ones.

One collector's bottom is another collector's top, and vice versa. A considerable amount of the antiques that circulate in any given category on Internet auctions do so between collectors of different levels. When the buyers outgrow the items, they will return to the Internet to resell them to a collector whose collection is the next level down from their own, and so on. Sometimes a novice collector will find a piece that is much more valuable than the others in their collection. Because the amount they can get for selling this piece is so attractive, some novices will sell off a high-level piece rather than have so much money tied up in one item. It should be remembered, though, that inexpensive beginner-level pieces in any category are one of the factors that attract new collectors. Enthusiastic traffic in lower level pieces in any given category on Internet auctions is a positive sign that this particular collecting category is vigorous and growing. This contributes to keeping prices strong all the way up the line. It increases liquidity and enhances the value of the collections of this type which are already in existence.

"A considerable amount of the antiques that circulate in any given category on Internet auctions do so between collectors of different levels."

The advent of the Internet has brought many changes which impact on how all kinds of sellers are able to sell, and the way that antiques are bought and sold has been forever changed. The benefits for sellers on the Internet are obvious. Websites allow sellers to sell around the clock, and around the world. When these sites are well-conceived, well-managed, and continually stock an attractive mix of merchandise that is well priced, these sites can become established sources for antiques buyers. Sellers who sell on Internet auctions participate in a dynamic marketplace where they can sell their items quickly and efficiently. Along with delivering an audience of potential buyers that can number in the millions, the other great news for all for sellers is that the Internet has gone a long way towards solving the issue of antiques liquidity.

THE BUYERS

Antiques buyers are a breed unto themselves. They pursue their chosen quarry with a zeal and dedication that is unrivaled. Some buyers delight as much in the pursuit of an item as they do in actually capturing it. As many real world antiques venues get drier, more and more buyers are being driven to the Internet. Buyers who buy antiques on the Internet can also be divided into several groups. They include pleasure shoppers, opportunistic buyers, cyber pickers, dealers, collectors, and supercollectors. Occasionally, a buyer can overlap more than one category. Buyers within each of these groups have their own psychology, and their own reasons for buying. Some venues are more appropriate for some buyers than for others. The Internet presents many opportunities for them all.

PLEASURE SHOPPERS

Pleasure shoppers currently comprise the largest group of antiques buyers on the Internet. These are people who are recreational shoppers. They enjoy window shopping and will buy whatever they find that tickles their fancy. They may have a small collection or two, but they are not serious collectors. Rather, they shop for antiques as a hobby. Pleasure buyers are not an easy audience for any seller to target, as it is impossible to know what they might see and decide that they like. They often buy items as fashion accessories, to complement their home decor, to give away as gifts, or just because they like them. In general, pleasure buyers tend, more than other kinds of buyers, to be impulse shoppers.

Online auctions suit some pleasure shoppers who enjoy the variety and the excitement. The adrenaline rush that occurs in the closing seconds of the auction just enhances their buying experience. However, some pleasure buyers do not enjoy the rough-and-tumble world of competing against dealers, collectors, and others. They prefer the leisurely pace of shopping through websites. Pleasure shoppers rarely shop from ads or bulletin boards, as part of their pleasure is the shopping experience itself. They enjoy browsing, comparing items, and the entire shopping process as much or more than they enjoy acquiring the item itself.

"Antiques buyers are a breed unto themselves. They pursue their chosen quarry with a zeal and dedication that is unrivaled. Some buyers delight as much in the pursuit of an item as they do in actually capturing it."

OPPORTUNISTIC BUYERS

Opportunistic buyers are a whole other kind of buyer. In the real world, they scour shops, markets, shows, house sales, etc. searching for any antiques which are sufficiently underpriced as to represent a bargain. Although they are buying to keep the items they find, they want the insurance from the outset that they have acquired their items at a bargain, and supposedly would be able to resell their purchases at a profit.

On the Internet, opportunistic buyers comb websites searching for misidentified and underpriced items, or obscure websites which may have been overlooked by other buyers. They also lurk in the background around closing time on Internet auctions, ready to leap in at the last moment when a bargain seems to be in the offing.

Opportunistic buyers are not buying for anyone except themselves. They are often knowledgeable about antiques to some degree, as well as current prices. This buyer can be flexible about what they buy, but the single criteria which takes priority over any other is that the item is poised to sell at a price that is significantly under the going rate for that item. Opportunistic buyers such as these want to collect antiques, but they only want to do so at a bargain, and they want the antiques that they tie their money up in to be priced at under the market values.

CYBER PICKERS

Cyber pickers buy opportunistically but not all opportunistic buyers are cyber pickers. The fundamental difference between them is that cyber pickers are buying expressly with the intention of reselling whatever they buy almost immediately, either on the Internet or to shops, dealers, or collectors. Opportunistic buyers generally buy with the intention of keeping their purchases or reselling them sometime in the future.

Cyber pickers maintain networks of contacts with real world dealers who specialize in various categories of antiques. The best pickers have a knack for finding objects and then matching them with the dealer who has a particular interest in acquiring that kind of object. Cyber pickers find items on the Internet and then resell them to dealers in real world venues. Other cyber pickers buy on the Internet and sell on it, too. They use the Internet to locate Internet dealers or other potential buyers who may want what they've got to sell. Some pickers take their chances and snap up whatever they find without having an eventual buyer in mind. But other pickers pick for specific dealers, or for specific items, and do not buy anything that is not on their shopping list.

Picking in real world antiques venues is not as easy as it sounds. To do it well requires a great eye, a lot of knowledge about antiques in general, an understanding of prevailing market prices, the ability to travel, negotiating skills, enough cash in hand to buy when opportunity presents itself, and a network of dealers and/or collectors who will quickly buy the items from the picker so that they can cash out and keep buying.

Cyber picking on the Internet relies on all of these abilities plus a whole additional skill set which includes a mastery of using the search engines, time to wade through website after website, and a certain tolerance for risk taking. Cyber pickers rely on their eye and their judgement. Sometimes their efforts are richly rewarded when a piece that was poorly photographed or badly described turns out to be a winner. Other times, they are not so fortunate. Cyber pickers have plenty of choices of how best to benefit from the Internet. They can buy a piece from an obscure website and resell it on eBay. Or, they can buy a piece on eBay and resell it to a local dealer. They can buy or sell locally or globally. Cyber picking can be a full time job, which will only grow as the Internet expands (or should I say explodes?) with even more antiques websites and Internet auction venues for them to buy from or sell through.

DEALERS

Some dealers who do not sell on the Internet regularly buy there. It is more convenient, the selection is larger, and they have access to items that they would not have found locally. These

"Cyber picking on the Internet relies on ... a whole additional skill set which includes a mastery of using the search engines, time to wade through website after website, and a certain tolerance for risk taking. Cyber pickers rely on their eye and their judgement."

dealers then resell the items they buy on the Internet in real world locations such as their shops, mall cases, shows, local auctions, or other local venues.

Real world dealers know that not every antiques buyer shops on the Internet and that there is a whole segment of buyers out there for whom an item purchased on the Internet will be fresh and new. Dealers who have customers such as these are gambling that their Internet purchases will attract a higher price in a real world sales venue than what the piece realized when it was showcased in front of a national audience of buyers. In some cases, they can be right, but not always.

A real world dealer never knows which of their real world customers also shop on the Internet. When the dealer is trying to sell a piece which exists in multiple examples this is not generally a problem. Even if their customer does shop the Internet, they do not necessarily make the connection between the piece that they are seeing in a real world venue and one that they saw on the Internet.

However, high-end or one-of-a-kind pieces which are sold through eBay and other Internet auctions can gain a notoriety among the small world of the high-end collectors in that field. When pieces such as these change hands in a transparent sale, high-end collectors and wannabes alike have grandstand seats to watch the progress of the auction and the eventual disposition of the piece. They note who bids, and who does not. They take careful notice of the hammer price, and of who elected to drop out of the bidding, and at what bid level they did. Some high-end dealers and collectors watch other high-end dealers and collectors and deliberately bid or refuse to bid on certain items depending on what the person they are watching does. The closing prices are noted, as is who was the final purchaser. Since so many of the top people in that field know of the transaction, high visibility pieces that are purchased on Internet auctions can be difficult for dealers to resell. Not only is it known what the dealer paid for the piece but also which collectors/dealers did not bid on it, or let themselves be outbid.

If a piece of this caliber does not meet reserve, especially after spirited bidding, many will conclude that the seller is pricing it too high. The seller is left in a difficult position because the piece has been widely viewed and has gone unsold. The seller can try to re-auction it, hoping that new bidders might emerge, or that some of the bidders who were outbid in the first auction might want another chance. However, the seller must also consider the fact that the piece has been shown to most of the people in their target audience, some of whom may assume that there is something wrong with it when they note that it failed to meet reserve. Bid histories which are available on Internet auctions make it possible for every observer to see not only who bid on an item, but they are also able to make conclusions about who chose to pass on the piece. Some dealers receive letters after an auction, and these high profile pieces are often eventually sold privately. Sometimes the final selling price is higher than the price that showed on the screen, reflecting a buyer who was willing to pay high, but who did not want everyone knowing that they had. Other times, the piece is finally sold at considerably less than the reserve, but the seller is spared the public embarrassment. When a dealer chooses instead to relist a high profile piece, they are taking a significant risk. Although a second auction can work to the seller's benefit and the piece will be sold, sometimes the bidding on a second auction is even less spirited than it was in the first auction.

Dealers who are buying items on the Internet with the intention of reselling them in real world venues are better off staying away from highest end, high visibility pieces. They will generally find lower to middle-range pieces easier to resell.

COLLECTORS

Collectors are a unique kind of buyer, and they have very specific buying habits. They are looking for pieces to add to their collection. Some collectors can be quite knowledgeable about what they collect, but some of them are surprisingly poorly informed. Different levels of collectors each have their own buying patterns.

Novice collectors tend to get their toes wet with lowest-level items in any one category, and they comprise the bulk of the market for this kind of item. A regular influx of novice collectors into any field is desirable. They help raise the level of interest in that field, and their enthusiasm can inspire others to begin collections of their own. In more concrete terms, novice collectors help to keep lower-level items liquid and to hold their value. As these novice collectors mature into middle-range collectors, they will demand better pieces. That growing demand will keep prices and demand for middle-level pieces firm, and in turn, exert pressure on prices of better middle-level pieces. Only pricing on top-of-the-line supercollector pieces will not be affected either way by whether novice collectors are entering that collecting field or not.

In truth, middle-level collectors aspire to own the best examples in their field but are rarely ready to make the financial investment required. Instead, many formerly novice collectors fill their collections with middle-level items and do not progress further. Sometimes, this is because prices for better items are beyond their reach, or beyond their desire. Middle-level items comprise the largest category of items sold on the Internet. The majority of antiques websites feature a mix of lower and middle-level items, and offerings in categories on Internet auctions tend to have a high concentration of lower to middle-level items.

Collectors can be especially picky buyers. They are more concerned with the condition of an item than are other buyers. Often they buy not only based upon the desirability of a given item but on whether that item will fit into their collection. In the old days, when collectors could only build their collections by shopping from real world venues, amassing a collection of anything was something of a feat. Because availability was such a problem, collectors often bought whatever they could find, whether they truly loved the piece or not. However, with the Internet offering heretofore unheard of levels of availability, collectors have many more options and are becoming more discerning. On the Internet, collectors are far less likely to purchase an item for their collection solely because they have finally been able to find one. Instead, they will consider the item's unique characteristics, its suitability for their collection, the item's condition, and whether they think the price for the item is a fair one. Most collectors are beginning to realize that they will always be able to find the items they seek on the Internet and that they now have the option of passing on pieces which do not quite meet their criteria.

SUPERCOLLECTORS

Some Internet catalog websites specialize only in the best of the best. Objects such as these are the domain of the highest level collectors — the supercollectors. This elite breed of buyer has the resources and the will to pay top dollar for something that they find on a website or to keep on bidding as if money is no object for a piece that they covet on an Internet auction. Supercollectors are focused, tenacious, picky, quirky, and driven. When they find what they want, they will do just about whatever it takes to possess it.

Selling to supercollectors is not always easy. They are more particular and discerning than middle or lower-level buyers, and because of the prices that they are willing to pay for items, they see it as their right to be so. Each of the venues on the Internet presents pros and cons when used to sell to supercolletors. Websites afford the supercollector an opportunity to shop unsupervised by other competing supercollectors. However, some will shy away from a piece which they suspect may have been viewed and passed over by other supercollectors.

A similar problem exists with supercollector-level items when they are auctioned on Internet auctions. Each supercollector who views it wonders why the others have passed it over, and they are loathe for other supercollectors to know what they have paid for a piece. If a supercollector-level piece goes unsold on an Internet auction, supercollectors assume that either there is something wrong with it or the price was out of line. Either way, no one will touch it with a barge pole! The seller is left with no choice but to attempt to sell the piece locally, privately, or possibly to place it with an auction house.

Should you come up with a supercollector piece and want to sell it, the best way to market it on the Internet is to try to find comparable pieces in Internet auction archives and note who the winning and second winner bidders were. Cross check their completed auction records as well. Then, decide which of these individuals appears to want this kind of item, and who, in the past, has been willing to pay what you want for it. Send them a JPEG picture of the item along with a polite inquiry letter explaining that you noticed that they had been bidding on a similar item and you have one of those for sale. The supercollector will appreciate the confidentiality. Some people will respond to your letter, even if only to tell you that they are not interested. Others will never reply at all. However, eventually your inquiry letters will lead you to someone who will buy it. Great items are too rare to go unsold, and demand far outstrips supply of them in all antiques categories.

However, in the event that your first few inquiry letters do not lead to a sale, by marketing it in the above manner you have not compromised the salability of your item. It has not been publicly humiliated by being "prostituted" (widely shown and obviously passed over by other supercollector buyers). Supercollectors have a natural aversion to buying prostituted pieces. One reason is that pieces at this level are usually highly recognizable as they are either unique or one of only few examples that exist. The piece is easily identifiable by other supercollectors, who can guess as to its provenance and what the buyer may have paid for it. Information of this type is not generally the kind of thing that supercollectors like to share with each other.

Most sellers will rarely ever have a supercollector piece for sale, but inexperienced dealers who market these pieces poorly can end up with a top-of-the-line killer item that they can't manage to get their money out of. In the end, they may be forced to sell it, at well under the market value, to an ecstatic middle-level collector.

In conclusion, buyers of all types are the biggest beneficiaries of the advent of the Internet. The Internet offers heretofore nonexistent opportunities for all types of buyers. They can buy at any time, choose from an almost limitless amount of items, and shop with ease and convenience.

CYBER ANTIQUES SHOPS

ONLINE CATALOG WEBSITES

Before the Internet, it was difficult for collectors who lived in small towns or rural areas to collect something exotic to their locale such as antique Japanese samurai swords. It was unlikely that they would find many (or any?) within their local area. However, through the Internet, this buyer can use the search engines to locate antiques dealers in Japan who specialize in them, as well as other Orientalist antiques dealers from Hong Kong to London and everywhere in between. Serious collectors can find pieces that rarely, if ever, come on to the market in their local area. They can also correspond with sword site owners and sword collectors around the world. This will often help the collector locate other sword collectors and other sites which are of interest to sword collectors. In addition, small collectors can compete on a level playing field with some of the top collectors in their field, as they both have equal access to whatever items are for sale, and they have an equal opportunity to purchase them.

Unlike trying to build traffic in a real world shop, Internet website sellers can be physically located in out-of-the-way places. As long as the owner can send and receive both e-mail and regular mail, then they can do business on the Internet. A website gives the seller access to everyone on the Internet who may have an interest in their merchandise from novice buyers up to the top collectors in their field, and those buyers may be located down the street or half way around the world.

When Internet commerce was in its infancy, buying from a website felt a lot like the wild west. There seemed to be no rules and no standard set of business practices had emerged. You paid your money and you took your chances. Sometimes transactions were satisfactory and sometimes they weren't, and there wasn't a whole lot of oversight or recourse in the event that buyer and seller could not work out their problems between themselves.

"Unlike trying to build traffic in a real world shop, Internet website sellers can be physically located in out-of-the-way places. As long as the owner can send and receive both e-mail and regular mail, then they can do business on the Internet."

Of course, unhappy buyers and sellers still have all the options that they have had from the beginning: their local small claims court, local arbitration courts, reporting instances of fraud committed utilizing the mail to the U.S. Postal Service, and the Better Business Bureau. But an unhappy buyer in Utah trying to work out a problem with a stubborn seller in Vermont could find that jurisdictional problems often precluded and that it would cost more for them to take legal recourse than they could possibly hope to recover.

However, as Internet commerce has grown into adolescence, standard business practices are emerging, and the increase in contact between both buyers and sellers through the various venues of the Internet has helped to identify and weed out some but not all unscrupulous sellers and problem buyers. Antiques buyers and collectors increasingly meet with each other on the Internet where information is exchanged and buyers' and sellers' reputations can often be checked out with others in the same field who may have dealt with them. Buyers, too, earn a reputation, and sellers can sometimes be forewarned by others who have had bad experiences with them. In other words, the world is getting smaller, and because Internet sellers and buyers are increasingly less isolated from each other, reputations can be both made and ruined online, and news can travel very quickly to just the people for whom it is important. In effect, and especially in specialized areas such as antiques commerce, this amounts to the online antiques community helping to police itself. The level of confidence that you can have in purchasing antiques on the Internet has vastly increased over that which existed just a few years ago, and as time goes on, it should only get better.

In addition, a few online professional dealers' associations have been established. Jewelcollect, a listserve which is owned by Liz Bryman and specializes in costume jewelry, has paved the way for professional Internet costume jewelry dealers by creating an online professional organization just for them. The dealers who have been invited to join Jewelcollect Registered have been approved for membership by their peers. They agree to adhere to ethical business practices; to register their names, addresses, phone numbers, and other real world information with Jewelcollect Registered; and to arbitration by Jewelcollect Registered if it is requested in the event of a dispute arising between them and a buyer that cannot be resolved by the parties involved. In return, Jewelcollect Registered provides its members with many professional benefits including a regular forum where pertinent information can be quickly shared between the members of the group. The Internet costume jewelry dealers who are members display their Jewelcollect Registered icons on their website homepages with pride. Not only is this icon an assurance for buyers who see it and know that they can buy from these dealers with confidence, it is also a compliment to the seller's reputation and the way that they conduct their business.

As Internet commerce continues to expand, online professional organizations such as Jewelcollect Registered will proliferate as other communities within the greater antiques community find that they are useful for networking and providing an added measure of confidence for potential buyers.

BUYING FROM A WEBSITE

Every day, many antiques sellers add their new websites to the more than 500,000 antiques and antiques-related websites already on the Internet. In addition, many of the antiques websites on the Internet are constantly being updated with fresh merchandise. Revisiting a site where you found nothing you wanted the first time might suddenly turn up something that you do. By conducting fresh searches, you will find the newest websites with even more chances to find exactly what you are seeking.

It is easy and convenient to buy from a website. Basically, you place your order by e-mail, receive an acknowledgment of your order including the address where your payment should be sent, send your payment, and once the seller has received your payment and it has cleared the bank (if necessary), then the buyer ships your purchase to you. Many websites provide an automatic order form, which is sometimes referred to as a shopping cart. For those which do not, if you find an item of interest to you, you should send an inquiry to the contact e-mail address given on the home page. Here is an example:

Hello,

I am writing to ask if item number TP-19 (insert a brief description here, especially if there isn't an item number; for example, "English Sterling Silver Teapot") on your website is still available. If so, could you please let me know, and tell me the amount that you would charge for shipping and insurance for delivery in the USA? I look forward to hearing from you.

Thank you,

Alice N. Wonderland

Because anyone can put up a website, amateur sellers compete with professional dealers, and sometimes the item descriptions on amateur websites leave a lot to be desired. Often amateurs are so caught up in adjectives like "gorgeous," "magnificent," "unique," "fabulous" that they forget more important information such as measurements and condition. In addition, some colors distort when they are scanned or digitalized, and a written description of the color is important. If you are unclear about any characteristic of a piece you are considering buying, write an e-mail to the site owner and ask for what you want to know, as in the letter below:

> *Hello,*
>
> *May I ask you a few questions about item number TP-19, the English Sterling Silver Teapot? How tall is it? How wide? How do you know that it is sterling silver? Is it hallmarked? Could you describe the hallmark(s)? How old do you think it is? What is the condition?*
>
> *I will look forward to receiving your answers to these questions so that I can decide if I want to buy this piece.*
>
> *Thank you,*
> *Alice N. Wonderland*

If you do not have any questions and just want to order, either fill out the order form provided on the site or send the following letter. You should supply the dealer with your complete shipping address at this point so that they can correctly calculate your shipping costs. It is also a good idea to include your phone number, in the event that the seller may need to contact you, as follows:

> *Hello,*
>
> *I would like to order #TP-19, the English Sterling Silver Teapot from your site. Please calculate shipping and insurance costs and send me the total due, along with the address where payment should be sent.*
>
> *Thank you,*
> *Alice N. Wonderland*
> *12 Buckle-my-shoe Lane*
> *Rabbitville, New York 00000-0000*
> *(123) 456-7890*

Some buyers prefer to write to sellers and make an offer on pieces that are for sale on their site. Many items for sale on websites end up being sold at a lower price than that which is shown on the website. It is the nature of the antiques business in general, and antiques sellers and buyers specifically that prices are usually not fixed, and that some haggling is permitted. However, don't expect sellers to give away their merchandise for nothing, and very low offers can be perceived by the seller as insulting. If you decide to approach a seller with an offer, make it a reasonable one for both of you. A typical approach might be:

> *Hello,*
> *I would like to make you an offer for # TP-19, the English Sterling Silver Teapot on your website. My offer would be $150.00 and I will pay additionally for the shipping and insurance. If this offer is acceptable to you, please include your address in your reply so that I can get your payment on the way to you.*
> *Thank you,*
> *Alice N. Wonderland*

The next decision the buyer must make is how to pay for their purchase. Some websites accept credit cards using a secured system or by providing a toll-free phone number where you can give your credit card information directly to the seller. Many website sellers prefer money orders or personal checks. If you still want to pay with a credit card, and the seller has stated that they are willing to accept credit cards, it is not advisable to send your credit card information in a single e-mail through an unsecured server. You could break the string of numbers into several groups and mail each one of them separately, but as e-mails occasionally get lost or hung up on a server and delivered several days late for no apparent reason, it is better to simply write and ask the seller to send you a telephone number where you can call them and give them the credit card information over the phone. The advantage to paying by credit card or money order is that once the seller has received payment they should ship your purchase(s) immediately. In addition, if you pay by credit card and find that you are not happy with the piece, some credit cards will allow you to stop payment on the item until a settlement can be worked out. Other cards offer insurance on your purchase. Check your credit card company's policies.

Money orders offer no such protection, but they are a great convenience for the seller and are useful for buyers who do not have a checking account. Money orders are available in many locations, including banks, convenience stores, and the post office. Paying with a personal check has the drawback that most dealers will not ship the item until they have deposited the check and waited 7 – 10 days for their bank to clear it. However, most websites do accept personal checks.

Once you receive the item, e-mail the seller to let them know that it has arrived. If there are problems, state them and suggest possible remedies. If there are no problems and you are happy with your purchase, let the seller know. This could be the beginning of a seller-client relationship that could go on for years to come.

SELLING THROUGH A WEBSITE

Websites are a great tool for sellers, whether they have a real world shop or not. A website is a low overhead way for sellers to showcase unlimited amounts of their merchandise to a limitless potential market of eager buyers. What factors make the difference between a successful website that gets thousands of hits per week, and a website that just sits there and doesn't seem to attract business at all? The answers lie in a number of elements including how the site is designed and constructed, how it navigates, how it looks, whether it is well stocked, whether fresh stock is regularly added, whether prices are fair, what else it offers, and that steps are taken so that potential buyers will be able to find the site. Successful website owners skillfully optimize all of these factors to create places that visitors want to return to again and again and online shops where they feel confident to buy.

The first step to creating a successful website is to scope out the competition. You should spend several months finding and visiting other antiques websites which sell what you intend to sell. By visiting these sites and analyzing them, you will learn all kinds of things, and benefit from their mistakes as well as their innovations. For example, sites which offer more than just items for sale tend to have more traffic in general and a higher rate of repeat visitors. Some of the ways to accomplish this are by including informational articles about antiques or other topics. A few websites include a virtual exhibit of photos of items potential visitors might enjoy seeing, and they change the exhibit contents monthly. Another plus are websites which furnish links to other sites which may be of interest to visitors. A website specializing in Depression glass might include links to Depression glass collectors' clubs, a Depression glass listserve, a book seller who stocks books on Depression glass, or other websites which sell it. In other words, if you do more than just sell, the chances are better that your site will encourage more visitors, and those visitors will want to return repeatedly.

Understanding the buyers' concerns will also help you create a website where potential customers feel comfortable doing business. Some sites do not disclose any personal information about the seller. Others provide the name, and sometimes the address and phone number of the seller. You should include as much personal contact information as you are comfortable doing. This would especially include your name, as it demonstrates to the buyer that they are buying from a person, and not some mysterious faceless online enterprise. You should include a page of terms and policies which should clearly state your return policy, shipping policies, methods of payment accepted, etc. You might want to include a page which clarifies for the buyer exactly what you mean when you describe the condition of your items. The important point here is to be open and up front. This will increase buyer confidence, and that is what Internet sellers need to do in order to make sales.

There are limitless ways to construct a website, but following these rules will give you a much better chance to create a successful one. The site must be constructed for pleasant, efficient browsing. Descriptions and photos must be clear and accurate, and properly sized. Merchandise should be changed or new merchandise should be added regularly. Policies must be spelled out in writing. And sellers should be prepared to service their buyers and not just sell to them. Most importantly, the seller must make the effort to advertise their site, and keep it registered with the major search engines.

People browsing the Internet are by nature impatient. They prefer to have sites load quickly. If a site loads too slowly, some people will give up and move on to another one, never having viewed the contents of the original site. Therefore, loading the site with graphics, music, and other devices which take up tremendous amounts of download time might not be such a good idea. In fact, it could cause you to lose customers. Instead, make a simpler presentation without needless graphics or music or other devices that slow down your site's load time. Also, steer clear of loading your site with pop-up windows, which most buyers find annoying.

Remember that people are visiting your website to see your merchandise, not a picture of your cat Fluffy wearing a killer pair of Haskell earrings, or an entertaining animated graphic of the cow

"People browsing the Internet are by nature impatient. They prefer to have sites load quickly. If a site loads too slowly, some people will give up and move on to another one..."

jumping over the moon. You wouldn't drag them aside in your real world shop to show them cartoons or a photo of your dog sleeping in that antique cradle that you have for sale, so why do that to visitors to your cyber shop? Most buyers have not come to your site for an "Internet shopping experience" including music, animation, and every other possible gimmick you can program into your site. They want to see the merchandise, quickly and efficiently, and if you slow them down too much, another seller who won't is only a click away.

Make your site easy to navigate. The home page should be clear, concise, and feature buttons to take the visitor directly to the category that interests them. For example, a site selling Art Deco might have the following greeting at the top of the page: "Welcome to Deco Delights, specializing in vintage Art Deco antiques." The following buttons might appear below the greeting on the homepage: furniture, jewelry, graphic arts, bronzes, pottery, glass, misc., policies, order form, and contact Deco Delights. Each of these buttons will take the visitor to the page(s) on the site where the items or information in that category can be found. In addition, the contact button is important so that visitors have an instant link for contacting the seller by e-mail.

Not only are many of your visitors impatient, they can also be lazy. Have the merchandise as few clicks away as possible from the home page. Visitors quickly tire of having to navigate through endless screens in order to reach what they are searching for. Web pages which are constructed so that the visitor has to reload a new page after viewing every few items are annoying and slow. Visitors vastly prefer that every item in a single category appear on a single page which they can scroll down without having to keep reloading every few items.

Your photos and descriptions are the most crucial part of your site. You must include color photos. It is virtually impossible to sell antiques on the Internet either on websites or in online auctions without them. Photos can be scanned or taken with a digital camera, but they must be clear and bright, well focused, and sufficiently close to the item so the buyer can see the detail. Additional photos can be added to show certain areas or features, but the first photo should always show the item in its entirety.

When designing your site, be sure that you accompany each of your descriptions with a thumbnail picture of that item next to the description. Sites which have lists of items for sale, but force the visitor to click on each individual item to see its picture are not pleasant to browse. Many will lose patience and leave, often without viewing everything you are offering for sale. Thumbnail photos allow the visitor to quickly and efficiently browse all the items on the page. Arrange your enlarged photo of each thumbnail to come up when the visitor clicks on the thumbnail.

Be sure to resize your photos. Thumbnail photos are fine for browsing, but any serious buyer will want to see an enlargement before spending their money. Don't make your enlargements unreasonably large, though. They can be strange and disorienting for buyers. It is not appropriate for a seller who sells antique thimbles, for example, to show photos of their thimbles blown up to 10" in height that take up the entire screen when the visitor tries to view them. First of all as they are very slow to download and you risk having your buyer leave. Secondly, thimble collectors are not used to looking at thimbles at this degree of enlargement. Not only is it inappropriate, but some pieces may not benefit from such intense scrutiny.

Many photo software programs allow you to tweak photos, by adjusting all kinds of characteristics including color, contrast, hue, tone, and intensity. Although these adjustments can rescue a photo that was taken without sufficient light or a photo in which the color has become distorted, tweaking a photo until the color on your screen matches the actual color of the item is a useless exercise. Unless every visitor to your site has the same computer and monitor as you do, the color will appear differently to each of them. And, what looks like brown to one visitor may look like mauve to another. Red, especially, distorts and it is important to include a written description of colors, i.e., cherry red, red orange, pinkish red.

On items where color is a critical determinant of value, tweaking the color, by altering or enhancing it utilizing computer software programs is simply not ethical. It can lead the buyer to expect something quite different than the true color of the item. For example, in the Bakelite world, clear leaf green is a far more desirable color than olive or khaki green. However, many programs exist which can turn a picture of a khaki Bakelite bracelet into a leaf green one, and vice versa. In most instances, the piece is worth up to 35% more if it is leaf green than if it is khaki. So, don't doctor your photos to make improvements on your items. Your buyer expects to get what you are showing them and not a nasty surprise.

Remember, it takes a certain courage to buy antiques over the Internet where the buyer does not actually have the item in front of them to examine. Part of your job as seller is to be your buyer's eyes and hands. Be truthful and honest in your descriptions. Whatever you write about an item is your warranty that the item is indeed as you have described. Therefore, it is critical that you research your items, know what you are selling, and do your best to describe it accurately and completely. Amateur sellers can make mistakes, such as misidentifying items, but the buyer never knows whether these mistakes are accidental or intentional. All they know is that when the item arrived, it was not as described or not as shown in the photo, or both. This gives the buyer reasonable grounds to return it to you for a refund. Therefore, to protect yourself as a seller, be very careful not to say anything in your descriptions or do anything to your photos which deliberately misrepresents your merchandise.

Concise descriptions are also in the best interest of the seller as well the buyer. When a seller writes that a piece is in perfect or mint condition, they have a leg to stand on if the buyer replies that the piece arrived and has cracks, chips, or other damage that may or may not have been sustained during shipping. Sometimes damage can occur during shipping. In that instance, the seller's claim that the piece was in the condition that they described when they shipped is an important point for them to make if, or when, they elect to make an insurance claim.

Sometimes sellers unintentionally make mistakes and miss small condition problems. If you have missed something that the buyer calls your attention to, be gracious and offer to work with the buyer towards a solution. You can always accept the return, but some buyers will be willing to keep a damaged item if you rebate them part of their purchase prices. Assuming that a rebate is preferable than a complete refund, try to work with the buyer to reach a settlement.

Some unethical buyers have been known to receive a piece, damage it, and then demand to return it, saying that it was damaged when it arrived. Other sleazy buyers buy a piece and then attempt to return an identical one that they already had which is damaged. A problem for antique jewelry dealers are dishonest buyers who buy a piece, remove the diamonds, replace them with stones made of cubic zirconium, and then insist on returning the piece. All of these actions by buyers are fraud and can be prosecuted criminally. Your best line of defense in these instances is your policies statement. If you suspect that your buyer is attempting to do something fraudulent, unless your policies state otherwise, (ie. "No returns" or "Items must be returned in the same condition they were in when shipped") then you may be forced to accept the return and issue the refund. This strengthens the argument that your policies statement is a critical part of your website and that you should be careful to write it to include all possible contingencies.

Your descriptions do more than tell the buyer about your items. They also give the buyer a clue as to how you do business in general and whether they can confidently do business with you.

Therefore, your description should concentrate on describing the item objectively and accurately. You should describe as many of the characteristics of the object as you can, and avoid lazy seller descriptions such as, "Magnificent Meissen plate! The picture speaks for itself." Well, it's true that the picture does speak for itself, but it certainly does not tell the whole story.

To begin with, descriptions which are replete with glowing adjectives such as "magnificent" and "stunning" are relying more heavily on pressure sales techniques than on describing the item and letting it sell itself. No amount of flowery prose is going to turn a mediocre object into a great one. When faced with this description, the potential buyer is left wondering exactly what is so magnificent about this plate in addition to what size the plate is, what the back marking(s) look like, if those flowers on the edge are accented with gold or brown as it appears on their screen, and they have no information about condition. Not many buyers will be willing to take the plunge and buy based upon a description such as this one.

However, if the seller accompanies the photo with the following description: "Meissen Plate. This plate is white, translucent, and is signed on the reverse with crossed swords in blue. It is hand decorated around the edges with pink flowers which are edged in gold. It is 8" across and has a single small flake approx. ⅛" in length along the rim." In this description, the object speaks for itself, and the seller has done their best to clarify anything that is not readily apparent in the photo.

Once buyer and seller have agreed on a price, the seller should send the buyer an itemized invoice including the final cost of the item, shipping method and charges, insurance (if any), and the address where they want the buyer to send their payment. In addition, this invoice should remind buyers that the seller will not hold this item for them indefinitely, and it spells out a time frame within which the seller expects the buyer to complete the transaction.

Dear Alice,

Thank you for your order from Deco Delights.

1 TP-19 English Sterling Silver Teapot $150.00
Priority Mail 3.20
Insurance 2.75
TOTAL DUE $155.95

Please make your payment out to Deco Delights, and send it to the address below. I will hold this item for you for ten days from the date of this invoice. I will e-mail you once your payment has arrived and provide you with a shipping date.

Sincerely,
T. Catinthehat
Deco Delights
47 Green Eggs With Ham Blvd.
Seussville, CA 00000-0000

Once you receive payment from the buyer and it has cleared if they pay by check, then it is time to ship them their item. Bear in mind that getting the item to the buyer in good condition is your responsibility as seller. Although most buyers include the cost of insurance in their payment, many website sellers offer to pay for the insurance themselves. Why? Because in the event of a loss it will be the seller who will be making the claim, and who will have to reimburse buyer for their purchase price, and often well before the insurance elects to settle the claim with the seller, if indeed they settle it at all.

Some specific kinds of antiques should not be shipped within certain areas during certain times of the year. Celluloid, for example, can warp at high temperatures. Winter months can be a dangerous time to ship fragile china and glass within sub-zero temperature areas. A dealer I know of in Ohio sold a very expensive Bakelite bracelet to a buyer in the northern Midwest in the middle of winter. The seller packed it properly and shipped it to the buyer. When the package arrived, the buyer was not at home to receive it, so it sat on her porch in sub-zero temperatures for several hours. When the buyer finally arrived home and brought the package inside, she was so eager to see the piece that she opened the package immediately, instead of leaving it alone so that it could gradually warm up to room temperature. Within minutes of being opened, the mint condition piece developed several internal cracks from thermal shock, reducing its value from thousands to less than one hundred dollars! The heartsick buyer returned the piece to the equally heartsick seller who returned the buyer's money and then placed a claim with the insurance company for that carrier. Because the package was completely intact and not damaged in any way when it was delivered, the insurer would not allow the claim, stating that the damage did not occur during shipping, nor was it the fault of the carrier. Rather, damage had occurred at the hands of the buyer. What a sad story for all concerned! The moral of the story is that under certain conditions some pieces may need special handling or other considerations so that they can arrive at the buyer's door undamaged. Be sure to discuss any applicable shipping concerns with your buyer before you ship.

Package your items carefully. There is no such thing as too much bubble paper, Styrofoam peanuts, etc. Bad packing can result in breakage or other damage during shipping. Very fragile items should be wrapped and cushioned inside one box, and then that box should be sealed and placed inside a larger box which allows 2–3 inches clearance on all sides. This cushioning area should be snugly filled with Styrofoam peanuts or crumpled paper, or other cushioning material. Be sure to seal all edges of your out-

"Package your items carefully. There is no such thing as too much bubble paper, Styrofoam peanuts, etc. Bad packing can result in breakage or other damage during shipping."

side box securely with packaging tape. You should write your name and address along with the buyer's name and address on the inside box as well as on the outside box. A good hint is to cover addresses written in ink with a strip of clear packing tape. This way, if the address gets wet during transit (not unheard of, I'm sorry to say), then the address will not become smeared and unreadable. Priority mail boxes should be taped closed on both ends. Rifling during transit can be a problem, and taping boxes closed is the simple way to prevent it.

Finally, ship items promptly. Once you have accepted the buyer's money, you are expected to pack their item and ship it in a timely fashion.

One fundamental difference between buying from online auctions and websites is that smart website dealers service their customers. If they don't hear from the buyer that their item has arrived and is satisfactory, they write to the buyer and ask. Sellers keep in contact with their buyers by making customer mailing lists and sending notices when they have gotten a piece that they think might be of interest to one or more of their previous buyers. And they are willing to answer general questions about antiques posed by visitors to their site. Every visitor is a potential customer. Being a pleasant and accessible seller can help to turn a browser into a buyer. Just consider answering those e-mails as good public relations, and definitely worth your time and effort.

Update your website frequently with fresh merchandise. Remove items which have been sold, and be sure to indicate when an item is on "hold" while you await a buyer's payment. Some websites feature a separate page for newly-added items which saves buyers from having to browse through all the items on the site. After a month or so on the new items page, these items are relocated to the pages in their correct categories. Smart sellers will then list a whole new group of items on their new items page. Having a new items page and keeping it fresh and well stocked keeps potential buyers coming back to your site.

Other sites e-mail customers when they update their site. Be sure to keep the e-mail addresses of your customers in a file. Although no customer would be pleased if you bombarded them with a constant stream of e-mail every time you added one or two items to your site, several e-mails a year announcing the arrival of fresh merchandise or a 25% off anything on the site sale will be welcomed and may help to drum up business.

Finally, the best antiques website on the Internet can languish in obscurity and receive not one visitor at all unless the site is properly registered with the major search engines. These engines help people find your site, but they can only do so if you tell them that you are out there.

Advertising your site is important, but not everyone on the Internet is interested in what you have on your site. Therefore, your advertising efforts should concentrate on reaching those you think are your intended audience. One tactic is to advertise your website in antiques newspapers or journals. Another is to post advertisements for your site in Usenet groups or listserves whose topics relate to the items you have for sale. Some site owners utilize Internet auctions to sell off merchandise and advertise their site at the same time. It is easy to add the address of your site or even a link to it in your auction item descriptions. Be sure to have your website address and your e-mail address on your business cards, too.

"...the best antiques website on the Internet can languish in obscurity and receive not one visitor at all unless the site is properly registered with the major search engines. These engines help people find your site..."

Including a links page on your site which has reciprocal links can be a great way to advertise your site and increase traffic. Write to site owners who sell similar merchandise and ask them to exchange links with you. By posting links to each other on each of your links pages, you can, in effect, pass customers on to each other. It is a mistake for an antiques dealer to think that this tactic is a foolish way for them to give away their potential customers to another competing seller. Especially in the antiques business, the object is what is of paramount importance to the buyer and not who is selling it! If a buyer finds something they want because they were helped by your links page, they may bookmark your site so that they can find that links page again. Who knows, they may even browse your catalog while they are there. And besides, your real competition for buyers is not from other websites but from sellers who are selling on Internet auctions.

INTERNET AUCTIONS

THE MARKETPLACE

In the past few years, Internet auctions have become a thriving marketplace where millions of dollars worth of antiques are bought and sold each and every day. They have enabled buyers and sellers who previously could not reach each other to meet and do business in an environment where everyone has equal access to the market and equal opportunities to sell or buy. A seller can sell as little as a single item or up to hundreds or even thousands of items, and buyers can choose from hundreds of thousands of items being offered for sale. The impact of Internet auctions on everyone in the antiques business is not to be taken lightly. Their existence and popularity have caused fundamental changes in the way that the antiques business works and have created heretofore non-existent opportunities for sellers, buyers, and others, and some troubling negative impacts for some.

The first to benefit from Internet auctions are casual sellers. Before the Internet, many individuals who had a few antiques they wished to sell had very limited access to the market. How could these casual sellers get their items in front of a wide audience of potential buyers? Casual sellers had few options — ads in the local papers, consigning their item in a consignment shop or to an auction gallery, sitting all day in a rented antique show or flea market space, renting a small case in an antiques mall, or trying to scrape together the money to open a small shop. Some casual sellers went to antiques shows with boxes of antiques that they hoped to sell to dealers at the show. Sometimes that worked, but often it didn't. In the end, if a casual seller wanted to sell their items, their only choice was to drag them from local antiques shop to antiques shop until they could find a dealer who was willing to buy them.

Because dealers ostensibly bought for resale, they insisted on paying low. But nothing prevented them from eventually selling the item to another dealer or to someone else for a hefty profit. In other words, lots of casual sellers were getting taken advantage of by the middle man in the transaction, the dealer, who often made more money on their items than they did. The Internet has taken the middle man out and made it possible for all sellers, including casual sellers, to deal directly with buyers. However, in doing so, it has placed dealers in a squeeze as casual sellers no longer need them. Individual sellers are the big winners on Internet auctions. They can list their item for sale and compete with dealer sellers and others for the buyer's attention and their bids. They are no longer hostage to conditions in their local antiques market or to selling low to local dealers. They now have direct access to buyers at a reasonable cost, and unless they have overpriced or misjudged their item, they can list it with a reasonable chance of success at selling it.

Most casual sellers are not business people. They are simply individuals wanting to sell a few items from time to time to any buyer who will buy them. Because many casual sellers are not antiques professionals, dealing with them can be difficult, especially

"Individual sellers are the big winners on Internet auctions. They can list their item for sale and compete with dealer sellers and others for the buyer's attention and their bids. They are no longer hostage to conditions in their local antiques market or to selling low to local dealers."

in terms of service and knowledge of what they are selling. They do not ship enough to be familiar with shipping costs or packing techniques, and they often tend to overcharge for shipping. They frequently do not package items securely or carefully, and breakage is a recurring problem. They can be frustrating to deal with as they are casual about e-mail and sometimes take days to reply to letters from buyers. In addition, they often miss condition problems on items that more knowledgeable dealers would spot, or misrepresent condition. However, occasionally casual sellers come up with fine items, and the irritation that sometimes accompanies dealing with them evaporates like a bad memory once the object reaches the buyer, and the buyer is pleased with it.

Another big winner in the Internet auctions are antiques pickers. Before the Internet, pickers walked a tightrope of buying without 100% assurance that they would be able to sell. They often had to tie up big money over time, which was not comfortable or good business, and then they had to hustle around until they found dealers or others who were willing and able to buy what they had found. Not any more! Internet auctions are a panacea for professional pickers, and growing numbers of them are utilizing online auctions as their single sales outlet.

Since Internet auctions place buyers and sellers in position to deal with each other directly, pickers no longer have to share a hefty chunk of their profits with dealers, and they are cutting the dealers right out of the action. By selling on Internet auctions, the majority of pickers have a very high likelihood that they can find a buyer for practically anything. This previously non-existent level of liquidity is especially beneficial for pickers, whose livelihood hinges on quick turnover of their merchandise so that they can continue to buy. Cash flow crunches, which formerly were the bane of a picker's existence, have turned into a problem of the past when they elect to sell on Internet auctions. In fact, when buyers pay promptly, the picker-seller can have their money back, plus profit, a short period of time.

There are stories circulating about a picker who rented booth space and stocked it with antiques at the huge Brimfield, Massachusetts, antiques market in the early summer of 1999. Anyone who inquired about the antiques in his booth was crispy told that nothing was for sale, that he had just brought them to show. Meanwhile, he went around buying items from other dealers, brought them back to his booth, picked up a digital camera, and photographed each item. Using a laptop computer with a cellular phone and a satellite uplink, he uploaded the JPEG's to a host area on the Internet. Then he immediately listed the items on eBay, literally within minutes of acquiring them! When many of the sellers he had purchased from learned about this, they were quite angry. Part of the reason that they were is because many of them do not participate in the Internet, and they suddenly had graphic evidence of what this was costing them.

Non-dealer buyers on Internet auctions benefit as pickers show them what they have found at the same time that the dealer-buyers see it. And since dealers by definition are buying for resale, non-dealers have a distinct advantage on Internet auctions. Non-dealer buyers can choose to pay that little extra that a dealer-buyer may balk at tieing up in an item, effectively knocking the dealer-buyers out of the action.

Although on many levels it would appear that Internet auctions are having a negative impact on dealers, this is not entirely true. Internet auctions provide dealers with a way to move stale or shopworn merchandise, or to sell items which are unmarketable in their present location. They help dealers to expand their sphere of buyers from a local one into a worldwide one. They put the dealers in touch with buyers who are interested in the items they sell, and savvy dealers utilize these contacts to expand their sales. They are also able to advertise their website or place of business in conjunction with their auction item descriptions.

Dealers on Internet auctions are competing with all other sellers. The advantage to doing business with dealers is that they generally know their merchandise, will probably describe it accurately, they are antiques professionals who are likely to do business in a professional manner, and their reputation is important to them. If a problem develops, a dealer, especially if they are well known within their field, is far more likely to try to make things right rather than risk having their reputation trashed online in front of a potential audience of millions, which will likely include many individuals in their specific field. Before you begin to participate in Internet auctions, it is important for you to understand feedback.

FEEDBACK

Feedback on buyers and sellers is available on most Internet auction sites. But how much responsibility do buyers and sellers feel that they have to other buyers and sellers within their Internet auction community? Is it better to conduct your dealings there following the adage "if you don't have anything nice to say, then don't say anything at all?" Or, as a responsible member of the community, do you feel that it is your duty, most especially when there are problems, to alert others?

The feedback feature on Internet auction sites was conceived of as a way for buyers and sellers to inform the community when transactions were satisfactory, or to alert others in the community about problem individuals. Ideally, feedback forums provide a way for both buyers and sellers to build a reputation which can be checked by other auction participants. On the face of it, it seemed like a good idea. However, a feedback system where individuals write their own comments leaves the system wide open to abuse. Some people will post polite relevant feedback, while others will abuse the forum to air personal grudges, engage in character assassination, or attempt to ruin another's reputation. Thus, along with their utility, feedback places everyone in the auction community in a somewhat risky position. No one edits feedback comments or checks to see whether they are deserved or not. If you receive unjustified negative feedback, there is little you can do about it.

Ideally, feedback on Internet auctions can be used to publicize successful transactions and praise buyers or sellers, or it can be used to warn others of bad experiences with a buyer or seller. By checking feedback ratings, a potential buyer can scope out a seller's reputation, and a seller can check out the buyer who has high bid on their item. However, feedback can be deceptive, or not tell the whole story, and should be read carefully. Many buyers and sellers who have been dissatisfied with their transactions do not leave feedback indicating that there were problems.

One reason for this is because often if one party has a bad experience with a buyer or seller and leaves them negative feedback, the (now publicly humiliated) buyer or seller sometimes responds with retaliatory negative feedback — whether it is deserved or not. These comments can be personal, ugly, and completely unjustified, but even when this abuse is reported to the auction representatives, it appears to be almost impossible to get these removed from your overall feedback profile. In the end, the person leaving negative feedback risks incurring undeserved damage to their own reputation. Internet auctions, especially eBay, have a long way to go to build safeguards into the system to protect whistle blowers.

Few buyers or sellers will have a perfect feedback record, especially if they have had huge amounts of transactions and hundreds or even thousands of feedback comments. With that volume of transactions, it is not unreasonable to expect a few problems to crop up. Internet auctions attract a wide variety of people. In more than three years and thousands of transactions as both buyer and seller on eBay, I have discovered that the vast majority of people who buy and sell there are honest and a pleasure to do business with. Feedback comments should discuss the transaction and not make personal reference to the buyer or seller.

Many little conflicts that erupt between buyer and seller are not reflected in feedback comments. The parties settle the dispute and keep it between themselves. So, when you read feedback on a buyer or a seller, take it with a grain of salt. Read the comments and use your judgement to decide whether they indicate that this seller is someone you want to deal with or not. Another tactic to use if you are still unsure of a buyer or seller is to search for others who have done business with them. You can always write to one or more of them and ask, confidentially, about their experience with that buyer or seller. Most will be willing to share their information with you.

"Feedback comments should discuss the transaction and not make personal reference to the buyer or seller."

An example of positive feedback left by a satisfied buyer for a seller might read: *"Item as described, responsive service, careful packaging. Recommended!"* Feedback from a seller left for their satisfactory buyer might say: *"Fast pay, good communications, an excellent customer."*

Leaving negative feedback can be risky. On one hand, you want to alert others to what has happened, but on the other hand, you must be careful of what you say. So, in the event that you are a seller and your high bidder never pays their bill, instead of writing: *"Dishonest sleazebag no-pay bidder. A piece of garbage all the way! AVOID!!!,"* write: *"WARNING!! No payment 1 month after auction close, ignores my e-mails."*

This somewhat milder negative feedback comment focuses on the transaction and does not make personal reference to the character of the bidder. However, don't assume that just because you elect to take the high road others will, too.

Individuals who leave negative feedback can find themselves in an unpleasant situation with an aggressively vindictive buyer or seller, and they can be in for a nasty surprise. Some buyers or sellers reply to negative feedback left for them by slamming the individual who posted it with repeated retaliatory negative feedbacks. These can be completely undeserved by the original poster. This is called feedback bombing, and it can lead to a feedback war. Meanwhile, the individual whose behavior earned them the original negative feedback is usually incensed and defensive because their actions have now been exposed to the entire community. They have been publicly humiliated, and their online reputation has been damaged.

Pleas to the auction sites' customer service department to intervene in a situation such as this may not be answered for several days. During that time, the irate individual can flood the original poster's feedback with negative comments. Although feedback bombing such as this is also a punishable offense on most Internet auction sites, in general, the site will not remove feedback comments, however obviously retaliatory. So, the damage that is done to the original poster's feedback rating in the interim can be permanent, as well as undeserved. Instances of punishment from auction sites for users who commit this infraction are all too rare.

So, mindful of these risks, if a buyer or seller elects to leave negative feedback, then they should watch their own feedback and contact the customer service people immediately if the object of their negative feedback posts retaliatory feedback.

As Internet auction sites mature, they have become more aware of the shortcomings of various feedback systems. In the future, look for them to explore alternative ways for buyers and sellers to rate each other's performance and share those ratings with the community, with less risk from retaliatory negative feedback or feedback bombing.

SELLING THROUGH INTERNET AUCTIONS

Selling items through Internet auctions is easy. First the potential seller must officially register with the auction site. This will usually involve supplying the site with your correct name, address, and phone number, and then selecting a user name and a password. Shorter user names are easier than longer ones, and sellers who specialize in a certain category might want to choose a user name that reflects their interest in that category.

The next step is listing the item for sale. All Internet auction sites provide their own online form for sellers to list their item for sale. Choose a headline for the item that best describes the item in a few words. Don't waste space with adjectives like "Simply Mahvelous" or "Gorgeous." Instead, choose words that buyers might use to try to find this item using a category or a keyword search. For example, instead of "Gorgeous Lalique Vase," the head-line "Lalique French Art Glass Vase" would be a much better choice. This is because buyers for this type of item would probably do searches on "art glass," "French art glass," or "Lalique." Although the former headline does describe the item, it would only appear if a buyer searched for the keyword "Lalique." Don't type in all capital letters, and avoid excessive punctuation and using typographical devices to get attention. Serious buyers are more interested in knowing what the item is, rather than vague but overstimulated headlines such as this one: "L@@K!!!!!!!!! GREAT ITEM!!!!!!" By the way, correct spelling is important in both head-lines and descriptions. If you misspell Lalique, then buyers who enter Lalique into the search engine spelled correctly will not find it, and those who do manage to find your listing will get a good laugh at your expense if your descriptions contain spelling and grammatical errors.

Few things on Internet auctions are more laughable than descriptions which go on and on about the extraordinariness and rarity of some item, only to scroll down to the picture and discover an item that is widely available at under $10! Also hilarious are misspelled, ungrammatical descriptions that ramble on about everything except the item for sale. Infuriating are the descriptions which say nothing other than, "the picture speaks for itself." Less reassuring are descriptions which do not state any sales policies or guarantees or a return policy.

So, fill out the description form completely and be sure that your description of the item includes its color, composition, measurements, maker (if known), any signatures or markings, age (if known), and condition. Remember that condition is very important to buyers on Internet auctions, especially since they can not handle the item before purchasing it. So, examine the item carefully and be sure to disclose any problems with the condition. One particularly amusing listing on eBay once noted that "....This item is perfect in every way except for the single large crack right down the middle..."! Actually, there is a market on Internet auctions for damaged items, but understandably, prices are considerably less than for comparable items in good condition. In addition, be sure that your description includes your terms of sale and your refund policy. Finally, if you have a website to advertise, say so at the end of the description. Keep your writing clear and concise and resist the temptation to wax poetic. Here is an example of a good description:

Lalique French Art Glass Vase
Light chalk blue cire perdue (lost wax) technique antique Lalique art glass vase. This vase is bulbous in shape, narrower at the base and widening at the top. It is patterned overall with grasshoppers and foliage. It is signed on the underside, in acid etched script, "R. Lalique." This same piece with the identical signature can be found on page 117 of MERCIER'S LALIQUE, ARTISTRY IN GLASS. *Approx. 11¾" tall, 11¼" wide. This vase is in immaculate condition with some evidence of wear on the base.*

After this part of the description, you should add your seller's policies. As follows is an example. Although it may seem a little long, it is better to spell things out and make your policies clear in the beginning rather than wait for a problem to come up.

Buyer to pay for shipping and insurance. The seller will accept personal checks, money orders, or VISA, MC, AMEX. Overseas buyers may pay with an electronic bank transfer in dollars. Seller's invoice to be acknowledged with buyer's complete mailing address within three days of auction close. Payment to be received by seller within 10 days of auction close. Items paid by check will be held for 10 days to allow check to clear. Items purchased with all other payments will be shipped immediately upon receipt. Items will be accepted for return if the seller is notified within 24 hours of receipt and provided that the item is promptly returned to seller in the same condition it was in when shipped. Refunds will not include auction fees or postage.

Although the above description is for an expensive piece of art glass, some descriptions can be very simple:

Pink Depression Glass Sugar Bowl. Petal pink Depression glass sugar bowl. "Tumbling Blocks" pattern. Mint condition but missing the lid. Approx. 2" high.

Follow this with your seller's policies statement and advertise your website, if have one, at the very end of the description. Here is an example:

Please visit my site at www.glassmistress.com *for more lovely antique glass, including Continental and American art glass and Depression glass.*

The next step is to add a photo of the item to your listing. Before you even begin working on the listing form, you must take a photo of the item and scan it into the computer, or take a digital photo and download it. The most commonly used format is JPEG. Then, your picture must be uploaded to a host site on the Internet. This is a site which will give your photo an address so that people can locate your picture and view it. Many ISPs automatically include a hosting area for their subscribers, so check with your provider. There are also sites which will host your photo for a nominal fee, and some which are funded by paid advertisers will host your photo free of charge. Dealers who own websites can host their own photos by uploading them to their site directory, where they will not be viewed by visitors to their site but will be available to be viewed by potential bidders when the photo's address is entered on the auction listing form.

Depending on the particular auction site, you must decide what your reserve is on the item, if any. Your reserve is the dollar amount that is your absolute minimum selling price for that item. Online auctions will not force you to sell an item for under your reserve. Many sellers use the reserve price feature to protect themselves and their investment in the event of computer outages or bids that do not reach the minimum price. Some sellers place a reserve on inexpensive (under $20.00) items. This can drive away bidders as most bidders on items at that level are looking for bargains.

Other sellers place unusually high reserves on their items. Once potential buyers notice over time that no bids ever meet reserve on items for sale from a particular seller, then they will gradually not bother to bid on any items from that seller. So, as a seller, you may want to give some thought whether a reserve is appropriate for every item you sell, and whether very high reserves are a good policy. After all, if your reserve is not met, you are welcome to contact the unsuccessful high bidder and try to reach a compromise price. But if you discourage bidders from even trying, then you are left with an unsold piece and no one to offer it to.

Remember, antiques prices realized on Internet auction sales are generally lower than dealer retail prices in metropolitan areas with high antiques activity, but they are usually higher than antiques prices in a small rural town. Therefore, sellers who used to buying and selling at New York City prices will find that they will not get New York City prices for items they sell on Internet auctions. They are competing with sellers from all over the country, selling comparable items — many of whom had lower acquisition costs for their items, and who are used to selling their items at lower prices. Either metropolitan area dealers must lower their expectations and fall into line with prices as they have emerged in each selling category, or their reserves will not be met and their pieces will go unsold. There is simply too much competition on Internet auctions for buyers to be willing to pay the highest retail price. Instead, buyers can and will ignore overpriced pieces and choose instead to bid on comparable pieces which are being sold at a reasonable reserve. In the buyer's mind, when compared to the high reserve and high opening bid pieces, these reasonably priced pieces seem like an especially good bargain.

Some sites also allow the seller to specify the opening bid and the bid increment. Some sellers use their minimum acceptable selling price as their opening bid combined with placing no reserve on that item. In effect, a single bid at the opening bid level will sell the item. This is a way that some dealers utilize Internet auctions to effectively retail their items. Although some buyers will buy items such as these, most buyers at Internet auctions are there to get bargains. When opening bids are set at the full retail price of an item, buyers are likely to pass over it and move to items that are similar and at a lower bid. Remember that you are competing with all the other sellers who have items in your category, and Internet auctions are set up in such a way that comparison shopping by potential bidders is easy and convenient. Be careful that you don't price your item right out of the action.

Bid increments are the amount necessary to move a bid to the next level. For example, if the bid on an item is $25.00 and the bid increment is $5.00, the site will not accept a new bid on that item for less than $30.00. By making your bidding increments minimal on less expensive items, you encourage more bidders to bid. By making them very large, even on expensive items, you will discourage some bidders from bidding. Some Internet auction sites allow you to choose the bid increment. Others, such as eBay, choose it automatically for you, depending on the opening bid and/or the reserve on the item.

Once you have completed all these steps, you can go ahead and list your item. Be sure to tag the item and write the auction number on the tag, along with the reserve amount if you have a reserve, and the auction closing date and time.

As the auction progresses, you may get letters from potential bidders asking various questions about the item(s) you are selling. Be sure to answer these letters promptly so that bidders have all the information they want prior to the auction close.

After the auction closes, you will be sent a notification from the auction website telling you who the high bidder was and the high bid amount. It is up to you to contact the high bidder with an invoice, within two days at maximum, as follows:

(enter the item number on the subject line of your message, along with a brief description) 291191160 Lalique Vase
Hello,
Thank you for your high bid of $699.00 for this item. Please include $20.00 for shipping, handling, and insurance, and send your payment to arrive within 10 days to:
Glassmistress Antiques
11 Mirror Way
Glassport, PA 00000-0000

Your buyer should reply to this invoice with a confirmation giving their name and address. Once payment arrives, if it is a check, you should deposit it immediately and contact your bank 7 – 10 days later to verify that it has cleared. If payment is by money order or credit card, pack and ship the item, and send the buyer an e-mail indicating that the item is on the way. If you do not hear from your buyer within five days of shipping their item, write them to inquire if the item has arrived and is satisfactory. If they reply that it has and it is, be sure to thank them for their business.

If the high bid on your item did not meet your reserve, you are under no obligation to sell it to the high bidder. However, sometimes buyer and seller can work out a private deal. Private deals which result from after auction close correspondences between sellers and buyers are another way to sell on Internet auctions. In addition, pieces which do not meet their reserve are not charged any auction closing fees. So, the sole cost to the seller was the original listing fee. This may give sellers more latitude to negotiate on more expensive items. Try sending the following:

(enter the item number on the subject line of your message, along with a brief description) 291191160 Lalique Vase

Hello,

Thank you for your high bid of $699.00 for this vase.

My reserve on this vase was $900.00, but I would be willing to compromise with you at $800.00. And, as an added incentive, I would be willing to cover the shipping and insurance costs. If you are interested in purchasing this vase at that price, please let me know within three days. If I have not heard from you by then, I will assume that you are not interested. I hope that we can do business together, and I will look forward to hearing from you.

Sincerely,

Glassmistress Antiques

Sometimes a letter such as this one will result in a sale. Finally, if your buyer has not acknowledged your initial invoice after three days, you may want to send the following letter to the next highest bidder in the auction:

Hello,

The high bidder in my recent auction number 135792460 has failed to contact me. When I looked up the bidder history, I noted that you were the next highest bidder.

Therefore, I would like to offer you this item for the amount of your bid, which was $78.00. Shipping by priority mail and insurance would add *$5.00 to your total. If you would like to buy this item at that price, please let me know within the next three days. If I do not hear from you by then, I will assume that you are not interested.*

I will look forward to hearing from you, and hope that we can do business together.

Glassmistress Antiques

DEADBEAT BIDDERS

Unfortunately, not all sales go smoothly. Every long-time seller has been faced from time to time with a "deadbeat bidder." This is an individual who is the high bidder on an item, their bid has met the reserve, but either they respond to the e-mail invoice from the the seller but never make their payment; or, the seller's invoice never receives a reply, and the seller never receives payment. The result is that the seller is stuck for the auction listing fees and the closing fees on this item. In addition, other bidders who might have purchased the item with no problems were shut out by the winning bidder's bid. Through no fault of their own, the seller is left holding the item, which is not what they wanted to do in the first place.

Some sellers make extraordinary efforts to gingerly coerce slow paying high bidders into paying up, while others are far more succinct. Some seller's posted terms of sale require high bidders to contact seller with their address within three days of auction close. They then require the buyer to have payment in their hands not more than 10 days after auction close, or they will nullify the sale and offer the item to the next highest bidder. Some sellers will send a first invoice, followed by a second invoice approximately one week later. If neither of these receive a reply, the seller sends a final invoice, indicating that unless the buyer contacts them within 24 hours to make arrangements to satisfy their obligation, the seller will nullify the sale, report the buyer to the auction administration, and leave them appropriate feedback.

Some sellers who follow all the reasonable steps to attempt to get the buyer to perform finally lose patience and alert the auction administration to credit their account for the closing charges on that item. When filling in the form, they check off the reason they are asking for credit as "Buyer never paid for purchase." This automatically enters a complaint from the auction site for deadbeat bidding against the buyer, and the auction administration will automatically send them a warning. Deadbeat bidding is a serious offense, and repeated instances of it can lead to a buyer being banned from some Internet auction sites.

Some chronic deadbeat bidders evade punishment by auction administrators by constantly changing their usernames and/or addresses. Eventually their behavior gives them away but not before damage is done to even more unfortunate sellers. One of the best defenses for a seller is to correspond with other sellers in their field and share information about deadbeat bidder experiences. They might want to check their high bidder's feedback for indications that they may have been problematic, such as negative or neutral comments. Another possible tool for the seller who finds a chronic deadbeat bidder as their high bidder might be a slightly modified initial invoice, as follows:

Hello,

Thank you for your high bid of $81.18 on my item number 1357924680. Including priority mail at $3.20 and insurance at $1.80, your total due is $86.18. I want to remind you that if I do not receive your acknowledgment of this invoice within 3 days, or, if I do not receive your payment for this item within 10 days of auction close that I will declare this auction null and void.

Please send your payment to:
Glassmistress Antiques
11 Mirror Way
Glassport, PA 00000-0000

Deadbeat bidders are not the only problem you may encounter when buying or selling through Internet auctions. Seller transgressions can include refusing to answer e-mail from successful bidders, refusing to complete a sale, misrepresenting items, incorrectly describing items, items not in the condition they are described to be in, careless packaging which results in damage during shipping, switching the item sold for an inferior one and shipping the inferior one, receiving payment but not shipping the item that the seller paid for, refusal to accept returns or issue refunds in a timely fashion, etc. Another problem that can crop up is buyer's remorse.

BUYER'S REMORSE

Buyer transgressions can include bounced checks, slow payment, slow or no responses to e-mail, and the famous "buyer's remorse." This occurs when a bidder purchases an item on an Internet auction, and then decides later that they just don't want it, even though the item is as described and there is nothing wrong with the item itself. Buyer's remorse can occur because the buyer has overspent themselves into a financial squeeze or got caught up in the excitement of the auction and in retrospect feels that they overpaid for the item. However, the net result is that sometimes buyers will send their payment, and after receiving the item, they will contact the seller and demand to return it, citing problems real or imagined with the item. When a seller knows that there is nothing wrong with their item, and the buyer insists on returning it, the chances are good that the seller is being victimized by a remorseful buyer. It is at the seller's discretion whether to refund or not in this situation, and it is no surprise that this might prompt the seller to leave negative feedback on that buyer.

Once your item is sold and has arrived safely to the buyer, both seller and buyer should leave positive feedback on each other if the transaction has been sastifactory.

Now that you know how to sell on Internet auctions, it is time for you to learn to buy from them.

BUYING ON INTERNET AUCTIONS

The first thing to do is find items that are of interest to you. The best suggestion is to visit several of the Internet auction sites and conduct a category search on each one. Go to the site map and find the auction site's list of categories. Once you have chosen one to browse, you can decide whether you want to scroll through all the listings in that category or do a search within that category to find the particular kind of items you are looking for. Category listings can be vast, and targeted searches within them are the most efficient way to find what you are looking for.

If you find an item which you would like to bid on, bookmark it on your browser (or place it in your "favorites" list). Read the description carefully, and note when the item is closing. If you have any questions about the item which are not covered in the description, write an e-mail to the seller and ask them what you want to know. Give them enough time to get back to you before the auction closes. Finally, before you bid, check the seller's feedback rating and review their most recent feedbacks.

Other bidders can be scoped out using tools provided on most Internet auction sites. Simply look up what other items the buyer has bid on and the list of items that they have won. Their buying patterns will quickly emerge. Those buyers who purchase only a few items that are often from differing categories or a buyer who buys for a period and then drops out only to return weeks or months later to buy again are all indications of a pleasure shopper. A list that includes many items in differing categories and a pattern of relatively continuous buying can indicate a voracious pleasure shopper, generalist buyer, dealer, or a cyber picker. Buyers whose list of purchased items are all from one or two specific categories are usually collectors or specialist dealers. Note the hammer prices that the buyer in question has been willing to pay. A buyer who is competing with you for a piece who has never spent over $100.00 on any single item will probably not return to bid against you on an item that has risen to over $100.00. However, this does not mean that another bidder who is willing to spend well over $100.00 might not appear in the closing seconds of the auction.

Trying to tease out information about the seller and other competing buyers can vastly improve your success at buying on Internet auctions. When considering bidding on an item, a quick glance at sellers' other auctions, and closed auctions by that seller, can give the buyer an indication of what kind of seller they would be dealing with. When there are few other auctions and they consist of a variety of items, then the chances are that the seller is a casual seller. If the list is long and contains many different kinds of items, then it is likely that seller is either a generalist dealer or a consignment seller. If the type of items on the list are all from a single category or two, the likelihood is that the seller is either a specialist dealer or a collector. Depending on what kind of seller this is, their reserve price will be affected, and some will have far more latitude to negotiate a price below their reserve than others.

In terms of reserves, those of specialist sellers and collectors will usually be the highest. Some casual sellers may not be knowledgeable enough to have correctly evaluated their items. Their reserves can be wildly undervalued as well as wildly overvalued. Sellers who sell through consignment sellers must raise their prices to compensate for the charges they must pay to their consignor, so consignor reserves may be marginally higher than those of casual sellers or generalists, but usually lower than specialist sellers or collectors.

All of this is valuable information if your bid on an item closes as the high bid but does not meet reserve or the item closes without a bid and you would like to contact the seller with an offer. Casual sellers, generalist sellers, and consignment sellers whose sole mission is to get the item moved out may be far more amenable to approaches from buyers than collectors or specialist sellers. Collectors are generally willing to keep their items and try again later rather than to sell them at prices which are below their expectations. Specialist sellers are like collectors but sometimes are in a cash squeeze or have other compelling reasons why they want the sale to go through sufficiently to bargain with a buyer. You never know what will happen until you write to the seller and ask, but any knowledge you can glean about the seller you are approaching may help you to work with them so that a deal can be negotiated.

BIDDING STRATEGIES

There are many different bidding strategies for Internet auctions. Some bidders will place a small bid when they find something they want, with plans to return later and put in their absolute maximum. Other bidders come in with their highest bid from the beginning, hoping that it will hold as other bidders bid against them for the item. A few bidders elect to wait for the last breathless moments before the auction closes to put in their bids. Their rationale is that it will be too late for anyone to come back in and top their bid. This kind of bidding in the last few minutes or seconds of Internet auctions is called "sniping," and it is not for the faint of heart.

Sniping requires nerves of steel, lightning fast reflexes, a reliably zippy ISP, and split-second timing! Sniping also carries with it several elements of danger. Among them, a coveted item may be

"...it is a better policy to put in your absolute maximum bid on the item whenever you choose and then sit back and cross your fingers and wait for the closing. Either you will win or you won't. "

lost because the sniper did not snipe in with a high enough bid, or another sniper sniped at the same time with an even higher bid, or the sniper came in too late and the auction had ended, or the sniper's ISP was not fast enough and the auction ended before the sniper was able to get their bid in, or the Internet auction had server problems which prevented or slowed down processing last minute bids, or the sniper just plain forgot when the auction was closing and missed it. The net result is that sometimes snipers are successful; sometimes they are not. I think it is a better policy to put in your absolute maximum bid on the item whenever you choose and then sit back and cross your fingers and wait for the closing. Either you will win or you won't. But bidding in this manner will prevent you from getting caught up in auction fever and overspending at the closing just so that you can be the winner.

THE AUCTION CLOSE

When the auction closes, you will find out whether your bid is the winning bid. If your bid has met the seller's reserve on that item (if any), then you can write to the seller immediately including your name and shipping address, and request an invoice and the address where payment should be sent:

Hello,
I am the high bidder on your item number 987654321 at $67.99. I will include $3.20 for priority mail, as indicated in your item description and an additional $1.80 for insurance. Please let me know where to send my payment.
Thank you,
Classy Glass Antiques
7 Steuben Avenue
Corning, New York 00000-0000

If the auction closes and your high bid did not meet the seller's reserve, and you still would like to try to purchase the piece, try writing the seller the following letter:

Hello,
I was the high bidder on your item number 987654321, at $67.99.
I realize that my bid did not meet your reserve, but I would like to buy
this item. Can we work something out?
I'll look forward to hearing from you.
Thank you,
Classy Glass Antiques

Some sellers will respond to this letter by stating their reserve, and offering you the piece at that price. Others will disclose the reserve but indicate that they are willing to take less money for the piece. Some sellers will not respond to the above letter, but will just go ahead and relist the piece on the Internet auction.

Once a transaction has been completed, and the buyer has contacted the seller to inform them that the item has arrived safely and is satisfactory, both buyer and seller should leave positive feedback on each other.

TROUBLESHOOTING INTERNET AUCTION PROBLEMS

When Internet auctions were in their infancy, they developed the tools for buyers to buy and sellers to sell, but they were sorely lacking in customer service. Internet auctions felt that their sole function was only to act as intermediaries who provided the venue for buyers and sellers to get in touch with each other and conduct their business. Once they had completed that function, they did not feel that they had any vested interest in the transactions themselves or that they owed the participants any further service.

Now that Internet auction sites, such as eBay, have matured, it is readily apparent to them that situations can develop which can require their intervention. In the course of conducting their business on Internet auctions, both buyers and sellers can run into situations where it is appropriate for the Internet auction site to be informed of a problem situation, to investigate that situation, and occasionally to take disciplinary action against a buyer and/or seller.

eBay upgraded their customer support by including Safe Harbor, which has an investigative unit that will address buyer or seller complaints and take action when they deem it appropriate. As of this writing, Safe Harbor's caliber of service has been disappointing. It is hoped that in the future eBay will make an even more serious commitment to servicing their more than 5.5 million registered users. At present, both buyers and sellers would be prudent not to depend on Safe Harbor as their only recourse.

Other Internet auctions are exploiting this eBay weakness by advertising that they are committed to customer service and willing to back up that claim with a responsive, conscientious customer service department. For individuals who have had unsatisfactory experiences with Safe Harbor, or any customer service on eBay, this might be an incentive for them to take their business elsewhere. But in the end, they will crawl back to eBay. In the long run, and despite their disappointing record of customer service, the only thing that could sink eBay is eBay itself. As long as they solve their hardware, software, server, etc. problems, and make more than a token commitment to customer service, eBay will remain the site whose size and preeminence in the Internet auction community make it the venue of necessity as well as the venue of choice.

"Internet auction sites have turned antique buying and selling into a convenient, profitable, and satisfying venue for many antiques buyers and sellers."

Internet auction sites have turned antique buying and selling into a convenient, profitable, and satisfying venue for many antiques buyers and sellers. Sellers, regardless of their location, can place their items for sale in places where they know their items are in demand. Buyers, regardless of their location, can choose from a selection of items which is far greater than what had been available to them prior to the Internet. In addition, buyers benefit from the level playing field that Internet auctions provide. Remember, on Internet auctions you have as much chance to bid on what is for sale as the top dealers and collectors in the world. He or she who is willing to come up with the highest bid gets the item. Period!

COLLECTORS & THE EMERGENCE OF SUPERCOLLECTIONS

Our penchant for collecting is a throwback to early hunter-gatherers, and collectors are modern society's hunter-gatherers. Today's hunter-gatherers hunt and gather for pleasure, whereas early societies primarily did so to survive. We are able to hunt and gather from a much wider area than our ancestors could have possibly imagined. Thanks to the Internet, our gathering range has increased to a global one, while our ancestors had to be content with what they could find within a few days walking radius. Unlike our ancestors, we are able to choose from an amazingly rich and varied choice of items. Best of all, technology has made it possible for us to hunt and gather without ever leaving the comfort and safety of our homes.

In the real world and on the Internet, collectors are the most consistently active group of buyers in any antiques field. These are people who never have enough of whatever they collect, and they can somehow always find the capacity and the money to buy more items for their collection.

For some collectors, their collection almost assumes an identity of its own at a certain point. Collectors add more pieces not necessarily because they want them but because they feel that the collection deserves to have them. They rationalize that the collection "needs" to have this piece in order to be more complete. However, by definition, a collection is almost never complete. Depending on the collector, a collection can become a voracious dependent which leaves the collector hostage to feeding and funding an addiction that in its most obsessive form is not unlike a drug habit.

The collector may be addicted to the adrenaline rush that they get when they find a piece that they want, and then pursue it until they make it their own. The pleasure high of a successful acquisition is short-lived, however, and soon the collector is off on the chase for another item. It's a vicious circle and can become a serious financial drain if the collector becomes truly obsessed.

In the days prior to the Internet, collectors were able to collect to the limits of what they were able to find that fit their collection. With the advent of the Internet, collectors can collect to the limits of their financial ability, and credit cards allow the collector to collect well beyond that. Before the Internet, collectors were limited in terms of the availability of what they collected. Often, they could not find what they wanted to buy. But by effectively destroying obstacles to availability, the collector is no longer constrained by availability. Most collectors who utilize the Internet to buy antiques will manage to remain moderate in their collecting habits, but it is a viable question to ask that with the unlimited availability that the Internet provides, some formerly moderate collectors may transform into voracious addicted ones.

As Internet use grows, not only within the current antiques community, but for the public in general, it is likely that collecting as a hobby will continue to gain in popularity. Internet listserves and other forums help collectors to network with other collectors. By mastering the search engines on the Internet, collectors can

> "As Internet use grows, not only within the current antiques community, but for the public in general, it is likely that collecting as a hobby will continue to gain in popularity."

easily find precisely the items that they seek. The Internet provides collectors with the widest possible area to search for the items they want and the opportunity to build collections of heretofore unimaginable size, range, and quality. Best of all, Internet auctions offer liquidity so that collectors can easily groom their collections by selling off items that they no longer want so that they can raise cash to buy more.

The quantity of antiques is, by definition, finite. Some kinds of antiques were produced in tremendous amounts, and the supply of them on the market will always be plentiful. Other kinds of items exist in precious few examples because they were not originally made in quantity or because they were too fragile to withstand the effects of time and use. As collecting continues to grow in virtually all sectors of the antiques business, and as more collectors find their way to the Internet and compete keenly with each other for pieces which are for sale, it is realistic to assume that eventually availability and prices will be affected.

The effects of antiques collector buying in these early years of Internet commerce will impact for years to come. There are three issues that are most crucial to understand when considering the effects of collector buying on the Internet. The central issue is the effect collector buying will have on available supply of antiques in their field. The second and tangential issue will be the effects that collector demand will have on prices. The third issue will be the emergence of the supercollections.

AVAILABILITY

Remember, collectors always have room for another addition to their collection and that their collection can number in the tens, hundreds, or even thousands of pieces.

Novice collectors will always be able to find novice-level pieces both in real world venues and on the Internet. Not only were pieces such as these manufactured in quantity, but they are plentiful and usually inexpensive. The Internet provides beginning collectors with the opportunity to build an attractive beginning collection quickly and at bargain prices. Eventually novice collectors reach a point where they either decide to abandon their collection or to expand and upgrade it. Sometimes they decide that they have enough of what they want, and some of them drop out of collecting. But other novice collectors progress through the novice collecting stage and emerge as more enthusiastic and more discerning middle-range collectors. Novice collectors who aspire to become middle-level collectors often groom their collections by weeding out their least desirable novice-level pieces and placing them for sale; increasingly on the Internet. This just adds to the oversupply of pieces at this level, so that it is possible that prices for this level of collectibles may fall even further.

Middle-level collectors are the single largest segment of any collecting group. This group is comprised of novice-level collectors who have made enough of a commitment to collecting and to their collection that they are eager to buy a better level of pieces than their original novice-level acquisitions. Middle and better middle-range items that are bought up by these collectors are "keepers." They disappear into collections from which they will not reappear for sale on the market anytime soon. These items have temporarily stopped circulating. Although some middle-range collectors groom their collections by selling off their bottom items as they move upward towards becoming higher-level collectors, many do not. Obviously since this results in many middle and better middle-range pieces being removed from circulation, the overall supply of them which are available continues to diminish. Because of the sheer numbers of middle-level collectors in any single collecting field, it is likely that in the near future, competition for nice middle-level pieces will be fierce. Not only will middle-range collector demand continue to grow, these kinds of items will be in undersupply. Collectors seeking better middle-level of pieces will face increased competition for them from upwardly mobile novice collectors and formerly disinterested high-end collectors who are "buying down" because of scarcity and high prices on better pieces.

Another long range effect that this situation will have is that it will force some buyers to change their buying habits. Demand will always exist for the best pieces from established high-end collectors. However, with fewer and fewer of these pieces in circulation, it is a safe bet that prices on them will continue to spiral upward. As these pieces become rarer and more expensive, higher-end collectors will "buy down." By returning to buying better middle-level pieces again because prices and scarcity have made the better kinds of pieces that they really want either unavailable or unaffordable. Upwardly mobile former novice-level collectors who are trying to "buy up" will find themselves in direct competition with established middle-range collectors, and both of them will be in competition with higher-level collectors who are buying down. It is obvious that supply of better middle pieces will continue to tighten, and as it is unlikely that supply of this quality of antiques in any collecting field will be adequate to meet the growing levels of demand.

PRICES

One of the hidden impacts of the Internet is that it is facilitating a major redistribution of antiques. The Internet's efficiency at getting antiques to the buyers who want them is going to cause shortages in some kinds and qualities of antiques. This will lead to spiraling prices in some qualities of antiques simply because demand for them will outstrip supply. It is a rational conclusion that prices on better middle-level pieces will move upward, even spiraling to unheard of levels.

The unique properties of the Internet facilitate and encourage market determined prices for antiques. They are a powerful influence on supply and are the driving force towards the development of a free market established price equilibrium in the antiques field. The principles of the free market particularly come into play on large Internet auction sites. Certain levels of collectors and the prices that they are willing to pay are becoming influential determinants on pricing within the ranges of prevailing prices in their respective collecting fields. And, it is the collector's consistent level of demand which has the strongest influence on the general level of liquidity of items within their field.

Another effect that the emergence of high prices will have is that they will encourage collectors to reassess the market value of the collection(s) they already own, based upon the new price levels. Appreciation in value is the hope of all collectors who hold their pieces over time. However, some fields of antiques will appreciate more rapidly and at better rates than others. Collectors should remember that although the overall price trend is for almost all kinds antiques to appreciate in value, antiques prices can be cyclical, especially on Internet auctions, and they should expect to see peaks and valleys from time to time.

Some of the collectors who bought aggressively in the early days of Internet commerce will make fortunes as their collections appreciate to levels that they would not have dreamed possible. However, as with all hard assets, these individuals will only benefit from their collection's appreciation once they begin to sell it off. Choosing the right moment to do so is a very delicate decision to make. As with the phenomenal skyrocketing of stock prices in the late 1990s, those who have stock have no idea when, or if, prices have truly hit their ceiling and the time to cash out has arrived.

"Collectors should remember that although the overall price trend is for almost all kinds antiques to appreciate in value, antiques prices can be cyclical, especially on Internet auctions, and they should expect to see peaks and valleys from time to time."

When a top-level collector pays an unheard of price for a top of the line item in their collecting field, especially on the Internet where the word travels at the speed of light, they have raised the bar for other collectors who aspire to purchase comparable pieces which may follow. Sometimes these historic prices are the result of a bidding war between two supercollectors, and subsequent comparable items will fail to meet that price. Although these prices seem shocking and excessive at the time, the potential price ceiling for the top pieces in any collecting field is impossible to estimate, especially because there has always been a very limited supply of the very best items, which keeps diminishing further as they disappear into collections.

SUPERCOLLECTIONS

The Internet has contributed to the emergence of more supercollectors. This unique breed of collector not only aspires to own the best of the best in their collecting field, but they have the financial resources to do so. They appear to have an endless capacity to continue to buy and buy, and they amass vast collections of incredible range, depth, and value. Utilizing the resources of the Internet, they can sometimes do so in an astonishingly short period of time.

I corresponded with a lady who already was a noted art pottery supercollector. One day when pickings were slim in the art pottery category, she picked up a fine piece of Art Nouveau jewelry on an Internet auction, intending to trade it away for more art pottery. She suddenly became infatuated with Art Nouveau jewelry, and within the space of less than a year, and buying most of her items on the Internet, she has managed to put together a supercollection of Art Nouveau jewelry which now numbers in the hundreds of items. Every single item in her collection is the best of the best. True, she is blessed with a level of financial ability that few collectors enjoy, but even if money were no object, she never could have done it, or done it so quickly, without utilizing the resources of the Internet.

The world of supercollectors is highly competitive. In any given antiques field, the supercollectors either know or know of the other supercollectors in their field. Not many pieces emerge for sale that are on the level of supercollector collections, so those that do are fought over tooth-and-nail. Supercollectors may not buy often, but when they do, they may spend thousands of dollars on a single item.

In conclusion, in terms of availability and prices, those middle range and upward collectors who have been slow to get onto the Internet may find that the window of opportunity for them use the Internet to an advantage in their quest to add quality pieces to their collection at reasonable prices may be closing rapidly. However, the good news is that the liquidity of their own collection has never been better.

THE ANTIQUES BUSINESS TODAY

Is the antiques business heading for a time when the Internet will become the dominant way that business is done? Can professional antiques sellers, both dealers and shop owners, continue to run successful antiques businesses without participating on the Internet? Are buyers and sellers being broken down into factions consisting of those who utilize the Internet and those who don't? Can real world antiques businesses and Internet antiques businesses peacefully coexist? Those who engage in antiques commerce today are faced with more choices, more challenges, and new realities. Understanding these new realities and how to utilize them for your own benefit is the key to successfully navigating the emerging landscape in antiques commerce.

DOMINANCE

The Internet is here to stay, and over time will increasingly dominate antiques commerce. But what effect is its presence having on the various stakeholders in the antiques business, and on the business itself ? As more buyers and sellers begin to participate online, there is an unlimited opportunity for continued growth of antiques-related traffic in all Internet venues. All types of buyers and sellers are finding that they can use the various resources on the Internet to their advantage.

Along with the unprecedented opportunities, the Internet is also causing some profound changes in how antiques commerce operates. As a result of these changes, there are unexpected negative impacts on certain groups of individuals in the antiques community. In fact, some of these impacts are affecting the fundamental nature of the antiques business itself. Although there will always be some individuals who will continue to elect not to participate in the Internet, the Internet will still affect them and possibly compromise their ability to continue to carry on successful real world antiques commerce. It is not just the amount of antiques commerce on the Internet that will establish its domination of the antiques business over time but the impacts which will be felt by everyone who buys or sells antiques, whether they do business on the Internet or not.

DINOSAURS

To begin with, it is unlikely that the Internet will ever completely replace dealing from real world antiques venues. The obvious reason is that many people will still elect to stay computer illiterate. Whether by choice or circumstance, they will let the parade pass them by. Despite statistics that indicate that over 40% of American homes have a personal computer, one inescapable reason why the Internet will never completely replace real world antiques venues, or any real world venue for that matter, is that not everyone will join the techno revolution.

There are a variety of reasons why these individuals don't participate in the Internet. Some do not take part because they either lack access to computers or do not have the computer skills, or both. Some people say that the investment in hardware, software, and the time involved in learning new skills, and paying for

"Despite statistics that indicate that over 40% of American homes have a personal computer, one inescapable reason why the Internet will never completely replace real world antiques venues, or any real world venue for that matter, is that not everyone will join the techno revolution."

an ISP is more financial burden than they care to assume. Another reason is that some people prefer things as they are, with real world items that they can hold and examine, and real world customers and dealers whom they can deal with face-to-face.

Some dealers are not participating on the Internet because of the way that they are used doing their business, and in their breadth of vision of what may be possible for them to do with their business. Some shop owners are still doing a profitable business using traditional methods and venues which include retail sales, antiques shows, mall cases, and auctioning goods through real world auction houses. They are getting enough traffic, and they are still managing to find items to sell from their usual sources. These dealers, especially if they do not have computers or computer skills, see little benefit in making the investment in time and money to participate in the antiques business on the Internet.

However, already on the market are new computers that are specially designed to convert potential users, such as these, who would want nothing more from their computer than ease of use including Internet access and e-mail capabilities. These new computers are priced much lower than computers with more features, and the prices on them will continue to drop, as will prices on software. (Much of what a user would need can be downloaded free from the Internet.) ISP prices are very affordable and coming down in some more isolated areas as ISP networks expand to provide better service to those areas. As for gaining the computer skills that are necessary, there are a plethora of books, videos, classes, and other aids available, and the skills that are necessary are not all that difficult to master. Computer anxiety is not a good excuse, and as hardware prices descend over the next few years, neither will be the cost of a computer. None the less, there will always be buyers and sellers who will buy and sell strictly in the old-fashioned way.

DEALERS

Of all the stakeholders in the antiques business, dealers have been the most significantly impacted by the effects of the Internet. The Internet has placed them in a position where they may be forced to change the fundamental nature of how they do business if they are to survive and prosper.

Many dealers complain that it is getting harder and harder to buy as the supply and distribution of antiques across the country is rapidly changing. With fewer items available for sale in their local areas, local competition for any item which emerges can be fierce and ugly. In the old days, dealers used to be able to sit in their shops and wait for people to come through their door with antiques that they wished to sell. These days, instead of walking their items into a dealer, people are selling their antiques themselves on Internet auctions. Pickers, too, are not taking their finds to dealers anymore. They, too, are selling them on the Internet. When items are sold this way, the dealer has been effectively cut out of the action and out of a possible profit.

The Internet's effect on real world antiques shops has been profound. The vast antiques shopping resources on the Internet have placed most real world antique shops at a considerable competitive disadvantage as their potential buyers can now comparison shop on the Internet. Shop owners who do manage to have items that buyers want to buy must price them including a percentage to cover their overhead costs. Before the Internet, buyers caved in and paid up if they found an item at a dealer that they wanted badly, even if they felt that the price was out of line because they had few other options. But these days, dealers are caught in the middle because it is likely that buyers can find comparable items for sale on the Internet, without significant overhead costs factored into the price by the seller. In today's global marketplace, this can make those real world dealer prices noncompetitive. Not every real world shop owner will eventually be driven out of business by the Internet. Those shops which are favorably located, well managed, and competitively priced can continue to be profitable enterprises. As long as they can be so, they will remain in business.

Another real world venue that is being impacted by the Internet are antiques shows and those who promote and sell in them. The Internet has placed the dealers who sell small lower to middle-priced items at antiques shows at a distinct competitive and price disadvantage. Their costs to participate in the show are the same as those of dealers who sell high-level pieces, yet their profit margin is considerably lower. Usually items comparable to what they are selling at shows are readily available on the Internet, and at a lower cost. Conversely, dealers who deal in higher-level items, priced into the thousands, often do much better with these items when they are sold at shows as opposed to being sold on the Internet. This is because buyers of items such as these are understandably reluctant to plunk down major money for a piece that they cannot see and handle. In this instance, antiques shows are probably a superior venue than the Internet for high-level pieces.

In time, this may lead to an elitism emerging in antiques shows, as middle and lower-level dealers whose very small profit margins and noncompetitive pricing can no longer support the overhead costs of shows. These dealers will gradually stop using this venue. This will mean that middle and novice-level buyers will find little at these shows that is at their level or that they are willing to buy.

Price is another issue. Until dealer prices at antiques shows in general come more into line with those prices as set by daily transactions on the Internet, many buyers will come to shows to look and then go to the Internet to buy. In the near future, the entire antiques shows industry, including the promoters and those dealers who participate in shows, will either make some necessary adjustments or watch as this venue becomes more of a traveling instant museum and sales forum for high-end items, as opposed to a sales venue that caters to all antiques enthusiasts.

The old days of finding an item, buying it, putting it in your shop, and then just sitting back and waiting for a buyer are over. In general, most dealers who buy and sell antiques in shops have perennial cash flow problems. As in every business, some of their cash outflow goes to pay for overhead, to service debt, and to pay for the costs of selling such as advertising, show booth rentals, or rents on mall cases. However, the lion's share of cash flow problems for dealers occur because they must continue to buy new inventory, regardless of whether their opportunity to do so comes at a time that is convenient for them or not.

Antiques dealers deal in a commodity that is unlike many others in that by definition there is a finite supply of antiques in existence, and only a percentage of them are in circulation and available to be bought or sold at any one time. Unlike other kinds of retailers who have merely to dial their supplier and place an order when their inventory gets low, inventories of antiques are not easily replaceable. Thus, antiques dealers must be prepared to buy whenever, whatever they want happens to show up, whether it is convenient for them to do so or not. Dealers tie up large amounts of cash in their inventory and have no guarantee of when, or if, any item will be sold so that they can recoup their investment. If they have bought poorly, dealers pay dearly for their buying decisions as their money sits trapped in unmarketable items. In addition, although antiques can appreciate in value over time, they pay no interest. Once an item has completed an unsuccessful run in a dealer's shop, followed by unsuccessful runs at one or more antiques malls, the item has become an albatross around the dealer's neck. Further, it is the nature of dealing in antiques that dealers buy pieces speculatively from time to time. If they speculate poorly on a regular basis, not only will they have a shop filled with unsold inventory, but they could create a cash flow problem which would sufficiently impoverish them and prevent them from being able to buy further, regardless of opportunities that may arise.

Until the arrival of the Internet, real world dealers had few options of extricating themselves from this dilemma. They could try to trade items to another dealer, perhaps from another locale. They could continue to lower the prices on these items in hopes that they would finally sell, or they could consign them for auction. But their cash remained tied up in the given item(s) until a willing buyer(s) could be found. Stale unsold inventory is a chronic headache for many real world dealers, and those dealers who still refuse to join in on the Internet will have to continue to deal with this problem.

Antiques dealers who deal strictly on the Internet can also end up with cash flow problems arising from buying poorly and having stale, unsold inventory. However, the major difference between them and non-Internet real world antiques dealers is that Internet dealers always have the option of cashing out on unwanted inventory by placing it for sale on online auctions with low or no reserves. They might take a loss, but more importantly, they have generated some cash from an item which was obviously a mistake and they were able to put that mistake behind them and move on.

So, there are benefits for dealers who sell in more than one real world venue at the same time. But if these dealers supplement those venues with Internet venues, they put themselves in the best position of all. Some dealers choose to keep their inventory in their shop but also have a catalog webpage which gives them access

"The various antiques selling venues on the Internet give antiques dealers options for moving out long-term, unsold inventory. Remember, inventory which is stale to a local audience will be fresh and new to the Internet audience."

to a much larger selling market than that which exists in the vicinity of their shop. Some dealers hold better items for their shop or mall cases but sell their lower-end items on Internet auctions. By carefully rotating their inventory from venue to venue, dealers can maximize their chances of selling it. The various antiques selling venues on the Internet give antiques dealers options for moving out long-term, unsold inventory. Remember, inventory which is stale to a local audience will be fresh and new to the Internet audience. Dealers who effectively manage their inventory can virtually eliminate the burden of unsold inventory, and the Internet can help dealers to dig their way out of at least some of their cash flow problems.

The sad fact is that some shop owners may be literally driven out of business by the Internet, although this does not have to be so. Rather, dealers need to be flexible and take a holistic approach in which they deal in antiques from both real world and Internet venues. This affords the dealer the expanded market and liquidity that the Internet provides while they continue to do business with their local clientele base which they have worked years to build.

Although some dealers will eventually close their shops in favor of dealing strictly on the Internet and other dealers may choose to supplement their shop business with dealing on the Internet, many dealers will continue to own and operate walk-in retail shops and not buy or sell on the Internet. The factor that may finally push some into making the investment in hardware and learning new skills will be the realization that they can do business on the Internet at a fraction of the cost of doing it from a retail establishment. Overhead costs are rising nationwide, and the bottom line is that selling on the Internet makes sound financial sense.

DEMOGRAPHICS

Another powerful reason why the antiques business on the Internet will continue to grow and expand is demographics. A significant percentage of antiques dealers and collectors are aging baby boomers. Some of them are beginning to think forward to their retirement, and others are possibly eyeing their shop and wondering when and how they will sell off everything and get out of the business. They are in a less acquisitive mood than they were in the years that they built their business. In addition, dragging their merchandise and themselves to shows and large antiques markets is increasingly becoming more of a physically draining hassle than they are willing or able to endure.

If these aging dealers can make money by spending their time sitting in their home or office in front of a computer monitor, then many of them will readily make changes in the way that they have been doing business. An added bonus for antiques dealers whose health is in decline is that by moving their business to the Internet, it will enable them to prolong the years that they are able to continue doing business, even if poor health eventually constrains their mobility. Dealers who want to semi-retire can float in and out of the Internet. They can take a few months off, and then reappear when they so choose. There will always be something for them to buy, or an audience ready to buy something that they have for sale.

It is a mistake to think that the Internet will eventually completely replace real world antiques venues. On the other hand, things are never going back to the way they were before. The Internet will play an increasing role in antiques commerce for the foreseeable future. As Internet participation continues to grow,

"An added bonus for antiques dealers whose health is in decline is that by moving their business to the Internet, it will enable them to prolong the years that they are able to continue doing business, even if poor health eventually constrains their mobility.

the Internet will exert an increasingly powerful influence on all sectors of the antiques business, and in all venues, both real and cyber. This has brought startling changes and long range effects that will reverberate well into the future. Today, the framework is being created for a whole new antiques commerce landscape in the future.

THE ANTIQUES BUSINESS OF THE FUTURE

INCREASED GLOBALIZATION & NEW TECHNOLOGY

Since the Internet has made all kinds of items available to buyers, regardless of regional factors, buyers from all over the world are now able to shop for the items they seek. Demand for antiques has always existed, often in places where buyers did not have convenient accessibility to the things that they would like to buy. The Internet continues to solve this problem by making antiques readily available for more and more potential buyers around the world.

Foreign antiques will be more accessible to American buyers, as will American antiques be more accessible for foreign buyers. However, it is likely that the increased outflow of American antiques from the United States will exceed the corresponding inflow of European, Asian, and other non-American antiques into the United States. By globalizing the market in antiques, without a corresponding increase in the overall supply of antiques, it is practically guaranteed that prices will rise in some categories of items as demand outstrips supply.

In the long run, one of the effects of Internet antiques commerce will be a massive redistribution of antiques around the world. Unlike the trend of the last two decades that had antiques traveling away from the periphery and into the cities, and from Europe to the United Sates, antiques increasingly travel the globe, often to areas of the world where they are exotic collectibles. This could lead to some surprises, as in the case of flow blue china and New Zealand.

Apparently flow blue china is very popular in New Zealand and commands high enough prices there that within the last few years a number of New Zealand pickers have criss-crossed the United States for months at a time buying every piece they can find. They ship container loads of flow blue china to New Zealand, where it is resold at prices that are significantly higher than those in the United States. The New Zealand antiques buyers cannot get enough of it, and American dealers and collectors, who are having a more difficult time finding it here, might eventually find a better selection of it in New Zealand or from an Internet seller who is located there. Other particular kinds of antiques could behave similarly, depending on the tastes of antiques buyers from around the world. As of this writing, American Depression glassware is becoming a trendy collectible within the French interior design and fashion communities.

One unexpected beneficiary of the global redistribution of antiques will be the foreign antiques collectors who for the last 25 years have watched with horror as their indigenous antiquities have flowed out of their countries. The Internet will enable some of these foreign nationalist collectors to repurchase some of these items and repatriate them.

There are many technological innovations on the horizon which will change the way that antiques buyers and sellers are able to conduct their commerce on the Internet. The most exciting of these will be the availability of high-speed connection lines at a reasonable price. They will eliminate tedious download times and enable a quality of transmission that is considerably superior to that which is available at present. Another innovation that will be perfected in the next few years is voice recognition software. In the future, this will save many from hours spent at the keyboard.

Online publishing will expand greatly in the future. Rather than purchase a book, you will go to a site, enter a code and your credit card information, and you will "buy" this book without ever having to take delivery of it. Instead, you will be able to access it online, any time you want, and as often as you want.

Online lending libraries will operate in a similar fashion. You will be able to choose books from their catalog and pay a nominal fee for a single access to that book, or perhaps for unlimited access to that book for a specific period of time. Either way, for a minimal expenditure, the largest reference library ever assembled in the history of the world will be available at your fingertips at all times.

Another exciting development will be the emergence of more virtual exhibitions and online museums. The main reason why many private collections are never seen by the public is because of security issues and the sheer cost involved in mounting an exhibition. By utilizing the Internet, such collections can be photographed and placed in the public domain where they can be studied and appreciated.

Home computer systems will increasingly utilize live videocams which will enable buyer and seller to meet face to face and for an object to be displayed in a more three-dimensional format. The facelessness that has characterized buying and selling antiques in these early days of Internet commerce will eventually evolve into face-to- face dealings, a more comfortable format for many people.

The world of Internet auctions will see the emergence of live real time auctions, where bidders on the Internet will compete with bidders in the auction house and other online bidders for items that are hammered down in real time. Live videocams will be used so that the Internet bidders are virtually in the room. Real time auctions that utilize this technology can have an audience of bidders that could number in the millions at any one time.

An extension of this will see the emergence of small companies who will travel the country with all the equipment necessary to set up online real time auctions from any location. These freelance Internet auctioneers will make it possible for a simple house sale auction in Kansas City, for example, to attract bidders worldwide.

The deluge of antiques which will make their way to the Internet in the next few years could give rise to oversupply on the Internet in some areas and a corresponding fall in prices in these areas. This may be especially true in lowest level quality pieces. It is possible that the low prices will serve as an incentive for speculative buyers who will snap up these items at bargain prices and simply sit back and hold them, knowing that eventually supplies will tighten. Once this happens, they'll sell and take their profits. Meanwhile, novice collectors will be encouraged and seduced by the wide variety and bargain prices on novice-level pieces.

"An extension of this will see the emergence of small companies who will travel the country with all the equipment necessary to set up online real time auctions from any location."

As the baby boom generation inches towards retirement, and their parents and others die and leave them inheritances which can include significant amounts of money, the scramble is on to find productive safe investments. One of the factors which has led to the unprecedented surge in stock prices in the late 1990s is that there was too much cash chasing too few safe financial instruments. As some stocks rose to prices completely out of proportion to the traditional methods of valuing a company (such as earnings price ratios), the value of some companies skyrockected, causing some Internet stocks to rise to astonishing levels on paper. Unfortunately, in the case of some Internet stocks, what they were selling is little more than air and potential. However, the usual dynamics of demand prevailed, and as always, there were winners and losers. It is possible that the money both made and lost on some of the

Internet stocks is more the result of speculation than a reflection of the true value of some of these enterprises. Smart investors will continue to search for opportunities to diversify their holdings by putting some of their money in less volatile investments.

Although it has been common practice for the last several hundred years for wealthy European families to place some of their assets in fine antiques, this diversification tactic is growing among wealthy Americans. One factor that has always discouraged investors from hard asset investments, such as high quality antiques, has been the constant problem of liquidity. The Internet has been particularly effective in changing the landscape in terms of liquidity, making antiques a more attractive investment for those investors who want to park some of their assets in a commodity that will likely appreciate. Internet investors can take possession of and enjoy their investment, and they can sell when they want to with minimum selling costs. It is possible that increased speculative investment in better antiques may result in them becoming commoditized, much like gold or investment grade diamonds, and a legitimate part of an investment portfolio.

We live in heady times. Instead of having to go out to find what you want, increasingly what you seek is being delivered to your door by the Internet. Things that you never thought possible to find are now available to you no matter where they are, or where you are. You are no longer constrained by time or location, and you can search for antiques around the clock and around the world. The Internet is the way of the future, and it is a delicious irony that commerce in the objects of the past is particularly at home on this vast and growing futuristic venue. Buying the hardware and mastering the skills to buy and sell antiques on the Internet will not only benefit you in terms of antiques but will give you the knowledge and confidence to roam the rest of the world of the Internet successfully.

ABOUT THE AUTHOR

Karima Parry has over 25 years of experience in all phases of the antiques business, from buyer to appraiser to auction cataloger to seller. In the mid-1990s, she opened Plastic Fantastic (www.plastic fantastic.com), a website specializing in Bakelite and other vintage plastic jewelry. She soon followed with a book, *Bakelite Bangles Price and Identification Guide,* and today she is considered one of the leading experts in this field. Along with operating Plastic Fantastic, Karima does consulting with Internet micro-commerce start-up firms as well as continuing to contribute articles on Bakelite and Internet antiques commerce to various antiques publications. You may reach her at this e-mail address: info@plasticfantastic.com.

COLLECTOR BOOKS
Informing Today's Collector

GLASSWARE & POTTERY

4929 **American Art Pottery**, 1880 – 1950, Sigafoose $24.95
5040 Collector's Encyclopedia of **Fiesta**, 8th Ed., Huxford .$19.95
1358 Collector's Encyclopedia of **McCoy Pottery**, Huxford .$19.95
2339 Collector's Guide to **Shawnee Pottery**, Vanderbilt $19.95
4726 **Red Wing Art Pottery**, 1920s – 1960s, Dollen $19.95

OTHER COLLECTIBLES

2269 Antique **Brass & Copper** Collectibles, Gaston $16.95
1880 Antique **Iron**, McNerney $9.95
3872 Antique **Tins**, Dodge $24.95
1128 **Bottle** Pricing Guide, 3rd Ed., Cleveland $7.95
3718 Collectible **Aluminum**, Grist $16.95
4852 Collectible **Compact Disc** Price Guide 2, Cooper $17.95
2018 Collector's Encyclopedia of **Granite Ware**, Greguire .$24.95
4705 Collector's Guide to Antique **Radios**, 4th Ed., Bunis .$18.95
3880 Collector's Guide to **Cigarette Lighters**, Flanagan $17.95
3881 Collector's Guide to **Novelty Radios**, Bunis/Breed.....$18.95
4652 Collector's Gde to **Transistor Radios**, 2nd Ed., Bunis$16.95
1629 **Doorstops**, Identification & Values, Bertoia $9.95
3968 **Fishing Lure** Collectibles, Murphy/Edmisten $24.95
5259 **Flea Market Trader**, 12th Ed., Huxford $9.95
4945 **G-Men and FBI Toys**, Whitworth $18.95
3819 **General Store** Collectibles, Wilson............................$24.95
2216 **Kitchen Antiques**, 1790–1940, McNerney $14.95
2026 **Railroad** Collectibles, 4th Ed., Baker $14.95
1632 **Salt & Pepper Shakers**, Guarnaccia..........................$9.95
5091 **Salt & Pepper Shakers** II, Guarnaccia $18.95
2220 **Salt & Pepper Shakers** III, Guarnaccia $18.95
3443 **Salt & Pepper Shakers** IV, Guarnaccia....................$18.95
5007 **Silverplated Flatware**, Revised 4th Edition, Hagan...$18.95
1922 Standard **Old Bottle** Price Guide, Sellari $14.95
3892 **Toy & Miniature Sewing Machines**, Thomas $18.95
5144 Value Gde to **Advertising Memorabilia**, Summers...$19.95
3977 Value Guide to **Gas Station** Memorabilia, Summers.$24.95
4877 Vintage **Bar Ware**, Visakay $24.95
5281 **Wanted to Buy**, 7th Edition...$9.95

TOYS, MARBLES & CHRISTMAS COLLECTIBLES

3427 **Advertising Character** Collectibles, Dotz.................$17.95
2333 Antique & Collectible **Marbles**, 3rd Ed., Grist............$9.95
2338 Collector's Encyclopedia of **Disneyana**, Longest, Stern$24.95
4958 Collector's Guide to **Battery Toys**, Hultzman $19.95
4566 Collector's Guide to **Tootsietoys, 2nd Ed**, Richter $19.95
3436 Grist's Big Book of **Marbles** $19.95
5267 **Matchbox** Toys, 3rd Ed., 1947 to 1998, Johnson.....$19.95
4871 **McDonald's Collectibles**, Henriques/DuVall $19.95

1540 **Modern Toys** 1930–1980, Baker $19.95
1886 **Stern's Guide to Disney** Collectibles $14.95
2139 **Stern's Guide to Disney** Collectibles, 2nd Series.....$14.95
3975 **Stern's Guide to Disney** Collectibles, 3rd Series......$18.95
2028 **Toys**, Antique & Collectible, Longest $14.95

DOLLS, FIGURES & TEDDY BEARS

2079 **Barbie** Doll Fashion, Volume I, Eames.....................$24.95
3957 **Barbie** Exclusives, Rana $18.95
4557 **Barbie**, The First 30 Years, Deutsch $24.95
3810 **Chatty Cathy** Dolls, Lewis $15.95
4559 Collectible **Action Figures**, 2nd Ed., Manos.............$17.95
4863 Collector's Encyclopedia of **Vogue Dolls**, Stover/Izen..$29.95
4861 Collector's Guide to **Tammy**, Sabulis/Weglewski.....$18.95
3967 Collector's Guide to **Trolls**, Peterson $19.95
1799 **Effanbee Dolls**, Smith $19.95
5168 Schroeder Collectible **Toys**, 5th Ed., Huxford $17.95
5253 Story of **Barbie**, 2nd Ed., Westenhouser..................$24.95
1513 **Teddy Bears & Steiff** Animals, Mandel $9.95
1817 **Teddy Bears & Steiff** Animals, 2nd Series, Mandel..$19.95
1808 Wonder of **Barbie**, Manos $9.95
1430 World of **Barbie** Dolls, Manos $9.95
4880 World of **Raggedy Ann** Collectibles, Avery $24.95

INDIANS, GUNS, KNIVES, TOOLS, PRIMITIVES

1868 Antique **Tools**, Our American Heritage, McNerney......$9.95
1426 **Arrowheads** & Projectile Points, Hothem $7.95
2279 **Indian** Artifacts of the Midwest, Hothem $14.95
3885 **Indian** Artifacts of the Midwest, Book II, Hothem.....$16.95
2164 **Primitives**, Our American Heritage, McNerney $9.95

PAPER COLLECTIBLES & BOOKS

1441 Collector's Guide to **Post Cards**, Wood $9.95
2081 Guide to Collecting **Cookbooks**, Allen.......................$14.95
5271 **Huxford's Old Book** Value Guide, 11th Ed. $19.95
4654 **Victorian Trade Cards**, Cheadle..............................$19.95
4733 **Whitman Juvenile Books**, Brown.............................$17.95

Schroeder's
ANTIQUES
Price Guide

. . . is the #1 bestselling
antiques & collectibles value guide on the market today,
and here's why . . .

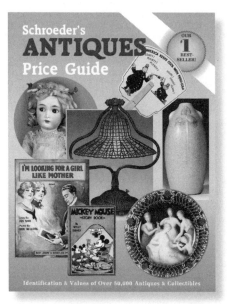